MOLA
TECHNIQUES

FOR TODAY'S QUILTERS

By Charlotte Patera

American Quilter's Society

P. O. Box 3290 • Paducah, KY 42002-3290

Library of Congress Cataloging-in-Publication Data
Patera, Charlotte, 1927–
Mola techniques for today's quilters / by Charlotte Patera.
p. cm.
Includes bibliographical references and index.
ISBN 0-89145-848-4
1. Appliqué – Patterns. 2. Quilting – Patterns. 3. Molas.
I. Title.
TT779.P376   1995   95-10189
746.445–dc20   CIP

Additional copies of this book may be ordered from: American Quilter's Society,
P.O. Box 3290, Paducah, KY 42002-3290 @ $18.95. Add $2.00 for postage & handling.

DEDICATED TO
La Familia de la Osa

ACKNOWLEDGMENTS

Anne and Howard Wenzel of Panama City for providing my gateway to the San Blas Islands and for their warm hospitality and many other helpful things including fun, food, and entertainment.

Anne Wenzel, **Bertha Brown Read**, **Isabella Lively**, **Herta and Oscar Puls** for sharing their vast collections of molas and making them available for photographing – and for many animated exchanges on San Blas adventures and information.

Charles Patera for the use of the Macintosh Plus, without which I would never write a book or conceive the diagrams and patterns to accompany it.

Herta and Oscar Puls for the photos of her works.

The Kuna Indians, who provide endless inspiration with their amazing techniques and creativity, not only for making molas, but also for living.

Jeronimo de la Osa and his wife Marienella Tajeda and their family for their boundless energy and hospitality.

Anne Sonner, editor, for adding cohesion to this book.

Kay B. Smith for design.

Whitney Hopkins for cleaning up and converting my illustrations into the proper software.

Charles R. Lynch for superb photography.

Michael Wicks for photographing Herta Puls' work.

Marcie Hinton for coordinating this whole project.

Photo credits: Charles R. Lynch, Michael Wicks, and the author.

CONTENTS

What are MOLAS?

Molas are panels of intricate-looking appliqué which are traditionally made by the Kuna Indians, worn on the fronts and backs of their blouses. This unique style of needlework uses several different types of appliqué, covering the entire fabric surface with vibrant colored outlines and surface details. Molas are constructed of two or three layers of fabric. The upper ones are cut into narrow lines or "channels" to reveal the colors underneath.

Misconceptions about MOLAS

The mere mention of the word "mola" automatically makes many quilters think of something "ambitious" or impossible. However, the technique is no more demanding than Baltimore Album, Celtic, or other types of appliqué. While needleworkers who make molas find them intriguing, many who haven't tried it are telling each other how difficult it is. The most expert Kuna Indians make very intricate and complex molas. However, the patterns and techniques in this book are simplified so that anyone with basic appliqué skills can have fun making a mola.

It is also generally believed that molas are made with many stacked layers of fabric and that pieces of the upper layers are removed to reveal the underlayers. This is a myth that has been repeated over and over by the uninitiated and believed by most who read or hear it.

Myths are difficult to destroy. I do not know who first started this one, but it must have been someone watching a Kuna Indian working who misunderstood what the Indian was doing. It can take many months to make a mola. Therefore few visitors to the islands can see all the stages of creating one.

Actually little or none of the top layer is removed in the construction of molas. Instead, it is slit and the edges are turned under, revealing the fabric underneath as narrow outlines which I call channels.

No large mass of the underneath layer is ever revealed. Four complete layers are used in some molas, but two or three are most common. Because there are many colors in some molas, people believe that there is a separate fabric layer for each color. The Indians are much more practical and logical in their methods. Most of the colors are small pieces appliquéd on or inserted under the top layer.

MOLA techniques in this book

My interest in molas began in the 1960's. At first I followed the popular belief of working from stacked layers, but after some frustration, I changed to the more practical technique of replacing complete layers with small pieces and inserts. As I learned more about molas, I realized that there are over 20 ways to make them. I began to experiment and taught myself numerous techniques.

Eventually I was able to visit the San Blas Islands. During my five visits to date, I have become aware of more variations of mola techniques and I collect molas with new mutations. My fascination stems from the fact that these primitive people live in thatched huts without running water or electricity, but have developed a unique craft that baffles most sophisticated needle experts.

In trying out many variations of mola making, I began to concentrate on the parts of the technique that I enjoy and eliminated many of the complex, time consuming details. I do not make molas in the true sense. I have made them for learning, teaching, or on commission, but I prefer adapting the Kuna techniques for my own uses for quilting.

This book focuses on the techniques that I have borrowed from the Kuna Indians and on discovering new ways to use appliqué or, as I like to say, "tricks with appliqué." My favorite pastime is exploring new ways of using what I have learned to evolve simpler variations and dramatic effects. I have developed a series of patterns for several styles of molas and have included a chapter on adapting mola techniques for contemporary art quilts. I hope you will be inspired to try out your own approach using methods from this book.

CHAPTER 1

THE KUNA INDIANS

PHOTO 1-1

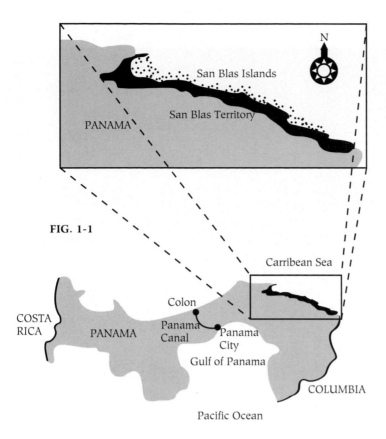

FIG. 1-1

also the time for doing the family laundry.

The living conditions on the San Blas Islands are fairly primitive. A few of the islands have water pumped in and limited electricity from generators. The Indians depend on kerosene for their lamps and stoves.

Transportation between islands is by dugout canoes. Most families have outboard motors, but you can find makeshift sails used with efficiency. There are general stores on the inhabited islands that meet most of their needs. Columbian trading boats come frequently, bringing other products and treats.

The Kuna Indians earn their income from raising coconuts on the uninhabited islands, from their farms on the mainland, and from fishing. The Kunas also earn income from mola making and tourism. Their diet is mainly rice, plantains, yams, fish, octopus, crabs, and lobsters, although most of the latter is flown to the city markets for income.

The Kuna society evolves around nightly meetings in the congresso – a large hut where announcements are made, laws are enacted, disputes are settled, and where rituals and recitations continue the Kuna traditions. Rules are set down for proper conduct.

Sports are an important part of the Kuna life. Softball competitions are held on the islands large enough to have a diamond and many islands feature basketball nets. There are schools with gymnasiums on some islands. Radios and rare television sets bring news of major sports, political matters, popular music, and I once had a glimpse of a soap opera from North America. I know of only one hospital on the islands.

When a Kuna marriage takes place, the young man moves in with the young woman's extended family. Because they bring new workers into the family, which increases the family's prosperity, girls are honored with a special celebration.

More Kuna Indians are experiencing the lure

■ **PHOTO 1-1.**
One of the Morris daughters with my favorite mola. Notice her fancy nose stripe. Nose stripes are thought to be cosmetic, a remnant of the ancient tradition of body painting, or to keep away evil spirits.

■ **FIG. 1-1.**
Map of Panama showing San Blas Islands. The San Blas Islands are composed of approximately 370 islands located between the Panama Canal and Columbia.

■ **PHOTO 1-2.**
Three generations of Kuna women. The red cheeks are often seen on the older women, made with a juice from the jungle.

There is some confusion about where molas come from. Most people mistakenly name countries from Mexico to Peru or "somewhere in South America." Molas are actually made by the Kuna Indians (also spelled Cuna) who live on a group of islands that are part of Panama in Central America. The San Blas Islands lie along the Caribbean side of Panama between the Panama Canal and Columbia. Kuna territory also includes a strip along the mainland of Panama (see Fig. 1-1).

Although Panama tried to get the Kunas to discontinue their traditions and to become modern, these Indians won their right to maintain their customs and traditions which are an important part of their lives. The Kunas are mostly autonomous and free from Panamanian domination. However, a Panamanian representative sits on one of the islands as "governor" to oversee the Kuna community.

Of the approximately 370 San Blas Islands, about 55 of them are inhabited. These small islands are lush with palm trees and other tropical vegetation. The Indians live on the islands near the mouths of rivers to have access to fresh water. Traditionally it is the job of the women to row over to the rivers to fill their plastic containers with water for the family each day. Plastic has replaced the large gourds used in the past. This is

PHOTO 1-2

PHOTO 1-3

of the city. Some of them leave the islands to live permanently or temporarily in Panama City. Each day small aircraft take the Indians and some tourists back and forth.

A few of the islands have simple hotels to accommodate overnight visitors who do not demand luxury. Scuba divers and recreational sailors are attracted to the islands. Cruise ships also bring in tourists for a glimpse of life on the islands and to experience mola shopping. Sometimes Kunas from many islands converge on one island to display a variety of exciting offerings when the cruising tourists visit. Each island decides on its own way of dealing with tourists – encouraging them, limiting them, or remaining remote.

Most Kuna women continue the traditional practice of making and wearing molas. They sew blouses with mola panels onto yokes in the front and back. Large puffed sleeves are added and a bottom ruffle or band completes the garment. Along with the mola blouse, the women wear wraparound dark blue print skirts and strings of beads tightly wrapped on each ankle and wrist. Red scarves are traditional headgear. Their handicraft has enriched the income of most Indi-

an families. Some mola panels are made specifically for selling to tourists and outside markets, but most often the blouses are sold or the panels are removed and sold from previously worn blouses.

Inspiration for the mola designs comes from everyday life, flora and fauna, sports, religious beliefs and myths, societal rituals, world news, and products from the city. Some traditional designs are repeated over and over. A clever person creates a new design which then is copied by other women. Apparently the original designer is not offended by this free use of her creativity.

Panamanian citizens have recently begun to appreciate the treasure they have in the Kuna Indians. Besides realizing that the Kunas attract tourists to their country, they have begun to fashion clothing with many details modified from these clever Indians' molas. Fashionable shops sell sophisticated attire with subtle mola trims enhancing shirts and dresses. The colors are very subdued and wearable. They even make molas for necklines, sleeves, and other clothing details using transparent fabric for the underlayer. T-shirts are glamorized with mola features.

PHOTO 1-4

■ **PHOTO 1-3.**
Kuna woman working on the small appliqué detail of two pineapples. Ali-gandi.

■ **PHOTO 1-4.**
Two young girls with their molas made with printed fabric which is unusual. It matches the print on the yoke.

■ **PHOTO 1-5.**
Kuna woman sewing her mola. Wichub-Huala.

PHOTO 1-5

CHAPTER 2

MATERIALS

FABRIC

The best fabric for appliqué is cotton broadcloth. A very fine weave is the easiest to work with. You may want to use a cotton and polyester blend occasionally, but it may not behave as well as cotton. Most quilters insist on cotton. Pima cotton is close to the cotton traditionally used by the Kunas, but is not easy to find. When fabric shopping, you will find some cottons that are coarser than others. The finer the cotton weave, the less bulk to contend with when folding under corners. Coarser weaves are good for the underneath layers or pieces that do not need to be folded and manipulated.

The Kunas work predominately with solid colors in bright and dark hues such as red, black, orange, yellow, blue, purple, and bright green. I used to prefer working with solid colors. Then I started to silkscreen my own prints with small subtle geometric repeat designs because I could not find many prints I liked. Now, so many exciting prints are available that I find myself using more prints to add more excitement. Use solids or prints as you like.

Beware of light colored fabric – darker colors can be seen through it. The folded under edges of a light colored fabric will be very visible when placed over a dark fabric. Depending on the transparency of your fabric, you may want to use only medium or dark fabric for the top layer of your mola.

Pre-wash fabrics to minimize future shrinking and color loss.

THREAD

It is important that the thread match the top appliqué piece, not the underneath piece it is sewn to. When a color cannot be matched exactly, I use a slightly darker shade of thread on medium or dark fabrics because it recedes, showing less than a slightly lighter one. If the fabric is pastel, a slightly lighter shade of thread is better when a perfect match is not possible. It is always a problem to determine what color thread to use on multicolored fabrics. Although invisible nylon thread is satisfactory, it is not as pleasant as working with cotton thread.

I use all kinds of sewing thread, both cotton and polyester. Mettler cotton machine embroidery thread has become a favorite because it is very thin. The thinner the thread, the easier it is to keep stitches less visible. Use machine embroidery thread in short lengths. Some thread may wear out and shred in longer lengths.

SCISSORS

Scissors are the most important tool for this cut-as-you-sew appliqué. Small embroidery scissors with *very sharp points* are essential. Sometimes it is necessary to stab and lift the upper fabric away from the underneath fabric for cutting the molas. Dull or blunt points will cause endless frustration. Keep your scissors well sharpened.

PINS

I use pins for most projects rather than basting. I prefer silk pins because they are thinner than other pins. I like to use the longer ones – 1¼". Thread gets caught on pins that have glass heads or other fancy shapes.

NEEDLES

I also like long thin needles. I prefer size 12 or 11, but they can be hard to thread. I use sharps, but I also like thin crewel needles because they have larger eyes for threading. Size 10 is the thinnest I can find in crewel needles.

Milliner's straw needles are excellent though they, like all thin needles, tend to bend quickly.

NEEDLE THREADER

This tool is helpful when threading a fine needle or when the thread gets limp with use and is difficult to re-thread. To use a needle threader, insert the thin pointed wire loop through the needle eye and then put the thread through the wire loop. Pull the loop back through the eye, threading the needle.

NEEDLE SAFE

A needle safe or needle keeper is a very thin case with a magnetic interior that keeps needles in place. A needle threader will also fit inside of it.

DRESSMAKER'S TRACING CARBON PAPER

This carbon paper is handy for transferring a design from paper to the appliqué fabric. To use it, place the carbon paper between the paper pattern and the fabric, colored side down on the fabric, and trace the pattern with a tracing wheel or pencil.

Several colors of carbon paper come in a package so you can choose one that contrasts with your fabric enough to see the traced image clearly. There is a type of carbon paper which makes marks which disappear in a limited time of their own accord. I do not recommend it since some projects can take longer than the visibility lasts. I prefer waxed tracing carbon paper. The unwaxed paper is so light in color, the tracing is almost invisible and therefore worthless.

TRACING WHEEL

A tracing wheel can be used to transfer paper patterns to fabric with the carbon paper. Some tracing wheels are serrated and produce a dotted line when rolled along the pattern line. The unserrated wheels produce a solid line. The serrated wheels can wear out the paper pattern sooner, but have the advantage of making a visible yet less prominent line.

LIGHT BOX

A light box is not essential, but it is very convenient for tracing as it eliminates the need for a tracing wheel and carbon paper. A light box has a drawing surface of stiff translucent plastic over a light source. The light shines through the fabric, so you can see the pattern underneath and trace it onto the fabric with a pencil.

PENCILS

A hard pencil (4H) may be used for tracing with carbon paper instead of a tracing wheel when the detail is too small to trace with a wheel. A pencil may tear the pattern sooner than a wheel. Use an ordinary writing pencil for touching up traced lines that start rubbing off the fabric before they are stitched. Use a sharp white pencil for touching up white carbon paper lines on darker fabrics. Some white or silver pencils sold to quilters are very hard and do not mark well.

PENCIL SHARPENER

It is essential to *keep your pencil point sharp* so that you can draw a fine, accurate line. A dull point makes a thick blurred line which will make cutting and turning under edges of fabric less accurate. I recommend using an electric pencil sharpener. I find many students do not keep their pencils sharp. However, professional draftsmen and artists know the importance of a sharp pencil.

ROTARY CUTTER, CUTTING MAT, AND CUTTING RULER

Most quilters find these tools a necessity. After you have finished your appliqué, cut an accurate, square block for seaming using the rotary cutter.

LAP DESK

For years I have used a lap desk for appliqué when not sitting at a table. I have one with a lid that opens to compartmented spaces for needles, threads, and all my necessities. It is handy for carrying if I need to, but mostly I keep it near a couch so I can work on my lap. It provides a rigid surface on which to fingerpress the edges of my appliqué as I work. It has really become one of my most useful pieces of equipment. A lap desk is not essential, but I highly recommend one.

CHAPTER 3

TECHNIQUES

PHOTO 3-1

The first part of this chapter describes the types of appliqué used in mola making. The second part provides basic instructions for preparing and stitching appliqué. Chapters 4, 5, and 6 teach you how to use these techniques to make the variety of mola-type patterns given in this book.

APPLIQUÉ IN MOLA WORK

Many needleworkers mistakenly think the terms "mola" and "reverse appliqué" are the same. *Reverse appliqué is a technique and mola making is a discipline that includes versions of reverse appliqué.*

Reverse appliqué is a technique in which the top layer of fabric is cut to reveal the fabric underneath. Reverse appliqué is negative (cut through) as opposed to positive (added on) appliqué in which a patch of fabric is sewn to a background. I really prefer the terms "positive appliqué" and "negative appliqué" over the terms "reverse appliqué" and "appliqué," but "reverse appliqué" is so commonly used, I hesitate to change it. Although many people believe molas are made of pure reverse appliqué, most molas also include other types of appliqué.

Reverse appliqué is not the prime characteristic of a mola, in my opinion. I believe that the main characteristics of traditional molas are:
• Filling all the space with detail or "horror vacui" (fear of empty space);
• Repetition of outlines.

The following are my terms for the different types of appliqué used in traditional mola making. All of these are tricks used by the Kuna Indians in varying degrees.

Reverse Appliqué Techniques
(Negative Appliqué)
Channel appliqué
Tandem appliqué
Inlay appliqué

Appliqué Techniques
(Positive Appliqué)
Double appliqué
Un-mola appliqué

Cutaway appliqué is commonly thought of as a Kuna technique, but the only time the Kunas cut away any fabric is when they replace the missing piece with another piece that will be covered with detail.

The Kunas also occasionally use regular appliqué, mostly for their trade molas that are sold to tourists.

■ **PHOTO 3-1**
Detail from the quilt, DAWN. This is an example of channel appliqué. (Full view page 16).

APPLIQUÉ IN MOLA WORK

Reverse Appliqué Techniques

Channel Appliqué
The top layer of fabric is slit and the edges around the slit are folded under and stitched to a foundation or background layer underneath, exposing a narrow opening or "channel." No pieces are removed. Reverse appliqué usually implies cutting and removing pieces from the upper layer of fabric, but this is rarely done in mola making. Chapter 4 describes different types of channels and how to make them.

Tandem Appliqué
One design is cut simultaneously from two different colors of fabric. The cutout pieces are switched and fit into the opposite pieces. The finished result is two versions of the same design in opposite color arrangements. Channels result in between the appliquéd pieces.

Inlay Appliqué
Small pieces are cut of many colors and fit together like a jigsaw puzzle over the foundation. When the pieces are appliquéd, channels are formed as narrow outlines between them.

Appliqué Techniques

Double Appliqué
Details are double appliquéd over the work in two steps. One patch is stitched down and a smaller matching patch is stitched over it so that the underneath color is revealed as a narrow outline around the edge of the upper one.

Un-Mola Appliqué
A narrow strip is appliquéd over the work. It resembles a channel, only the image is positive rather than negative. I call this technique "un-mola" facetiously because it is not a reverse appliqué technique which most people expect to see in molas.

■ **PHOTO 3-2.**
DAWN, 64" x 64", 1982. In the quilt, DAWN, I combined channel appliqué and cutaway appliqué. Each design was done twice, once with cutaway appliqué, and once with channel appliqué. Fig. 3-1 and Fig. 3-2 show how to do these two types of appliqué. After I made this quilt in 1982, I became more fascinated with the actual mola techniques. I decided I preferred channel appliqué used in the traditional molas and stopped doing much cutaway appliqué. (Detail, page 14).

■ **FIG. 3-1.**
Channel appliqué is appliqué in which a slit is made in the top fabric, edges folded under and stitched to form a narrow groove or "channel," revealing the underneath fabric.

■ **FIG. 3-2.**
Cutaway appliqué.

PHOTO 3-2

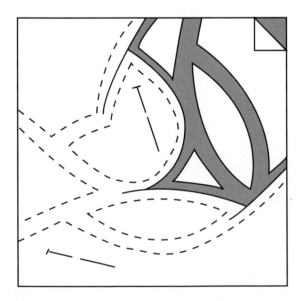

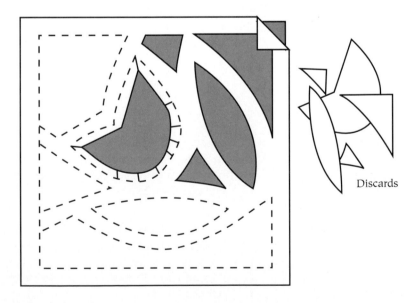

Discards

FIG. 3-1   **FIG. 3-2**

PREPARING AND STITCHING APPLIQUÉ

Sizing

Allow enough space around the design so that you can seam it to other pieces for making a quilt, pillow, garment, or a wall hanging. I also suggest oversizing the piece a little to allow for any drawing up that can occur as you do the appliqué work. Everyone works at a different tension and the mola can shrink unpredictably as you work it. Do the final trimming of a block after the appliqué is complete and pressed.

Tracing

When tracing your pattern, position it so there is ample fabric around the final piece as mentioned above. Always pin the pattern to the fabric, allowing space for the dressmaker's carbon paper to be moved if it is smaller than the design. While tracing, bear down hard with the tracing wheel or pencil. Check before you trace the entire design to make sure that you are getting a good permanent image. If not, switch to a more contrasting color of carbon paper or press harder.

If you have a light box, tracing carbon is not needed. Tape the pattern with the fabric over it to the light box surface. You can also use a window in the daytime for tracing by taping the fabric over the pattern on the glass. Use a sharp writing pencil to trace your pattern.

If your fabric is light enough in color, you can place it over the pattern and see the image through it, eliminating the need for the carbon paper or a light box. Then use a sharp writing pencil to trace the design.

For variety in your work, you may want to reverse the pattern so that a figure will face the opposite direction (Fig. 3-3 through Fig. 3-6). There are several ways to do this. The easiest way is to use a light box (Fig. 3-4). Just flip the pattern over and trace it onto the fabric. The light box makes the fabric and pattern paper transparent so that the pattern is visible through it. When using dressmaker's carbon (Fig. 3-5), after one tracing, the image will be clearly indented on the reverse side of the pattern. The pattern can then be flipped over and traced with the reverse side up. If the pattern has not been used, another way to transfer a reverse image is to trace on the following "sandwich": the pattern on top of the fabric which is *wrong side up*, on top of the carbon paper which is *carbon side up* (Fig. 3-6). The image will be reversed on the right side of the fabric.

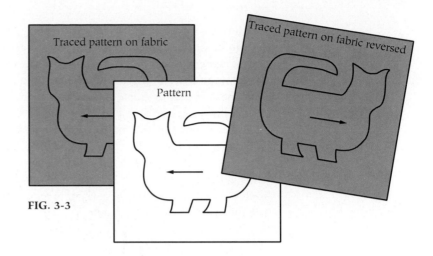

FIG. 3-3

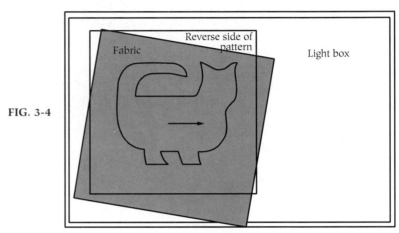

FIG. 3-4

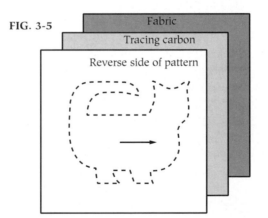

FIG. 3-5

■ **FIG. 3-3 through 3-6.** *Reversing the pattern so that a figure will face the opposite direction.*

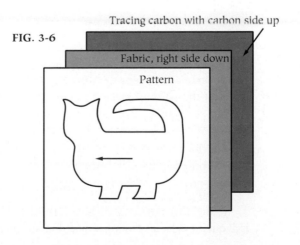

FIG. 3-6

If you want to extend a geometric repeat pattern to create a larger piece, after you trace a repeat pattern once, move the pattern over on the fabric so that the edges of the pattern line up with those traced to create a continuous extension of the design without a visible break.

The patterns in this book are presented in two ways. For the PRIMITIVE CRITTERS and FLOWERS DECO patterns, the lines on the patterns indicate where to *cut*. For the other patterns in this book, the lines indicate where to *fold*. Follow the instructions on each pattern.

FIG. 3-7

■ **FIG. 3-7.**
Patterns are presented in two ways. Left, lines on the patterns indicate where to cut. Right, lines indicate where to fold. Each pattern will indicate method to be used.

Pinning
Pin the upper layer of fabric to the lower layer. You do not need many pins. As you work, keep moving pins around to secure cut parts that become loose. You may prefer to baste instead of pinning to secure the pieces together, but pins are handier for securing cut pieces as you work.

APPLIQUÉ METHODS
Templates, freezer paper, and preliminary pressing of edges under are not practical techniques for this mola appliqué which is based on the cut-as-you-go method. I will describe the way I prefer to work. You may find it more comfortable to proceed in other ways. Whatever works for you is best.

Decide which way of working is most comfortable for you. First place the work on a flat surface such as a table or lap desk and stitch it in that position. This keeps the work flat and gravity holds all the parts in place. Then try picking up the work in your hands. I find that long straight edges are easier to start on the table and that tricky corners and details are easier when picking it up. I suggest using both methods together.

Cutting
I use the cut-as-you-go method for all appliqué. It calls for cutting a little and stitching a little, rather than pre-cutting the entire design. With this method, no parts will get out of place until you cut them. The exception is tandem appliqué in which the entire design is cut before sewing.

For some of the patterns, cut on the traced line. For others, cut between the fold lines. Follow the instructions on each pattern.

Stitching Technique
(Instructions for right-handed stitchers)
I recommend cutting a thread about 18 to 20 inches in length. Using too long a piece can result in the thread getting knotted, tangled, limp or wearing out quickly.

1. Knot your thread and bring the needle up through the top layer of fabric on the fold line, hiding the knot under the fabric (Fig. 3-8).

2. Working on a flat surface, use your fingers to fold the edge under, holding the edge under with your left finger or thumb. Fold under an inch or two along the fold edge and finger-press it (Fig. 3-9). Hold the piece with the folded edge toward yourself.

Some students feel it necessary to pin the folded edge with many pins close together. So many pins are unnecessary and thread gets caught on them. Learn to fold, hold and stitch the edge under as you work. With practice, you will find no need to pin the edges.

3. Insert the needle down through the base or foundation fabric right above where you brought it up through the top fabric. Bring the needle up about ⅛" or less from the first stitch through both fabrics on the folded edge to start the next stitch (Fig. 3-10).

4. Make your stitches about ⅛" or less apart. Keep them even in size and spacing (Fig. 3-11). Keep turning the work as necessary to a comfortable position, folding the edge under toward yourself. Some people learn to appliqué the opposite way, folding the fabric away from themselves. I find I have better control if I turn the edge toward myself, but use the method you prefer.

5. To work the outward corners, first clip off a bit of the corner to get rid of the bulk (Fig. 3-12a). Then stitch one edge, placing *two stitches* on the corner, one over the other, to anchor it securely (Fig. 3-12b). Fold the adjacent edge

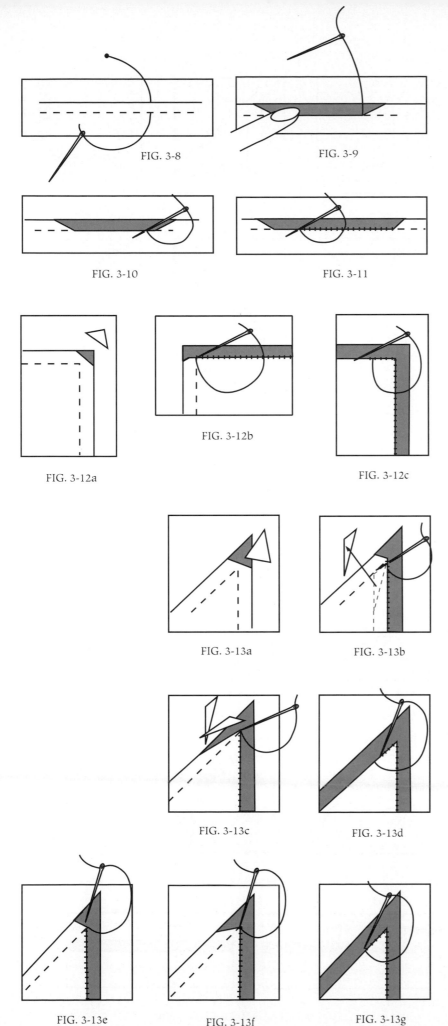

FIG. 3-8

FIG. 3-9

FIG. 3-10

FIG. 3-11

FIG. 3-12a

FIG. 3-12b

FIG. 3-12c

FIG. 3-13a

FIG. 3-13b

FIG. 3-13c

FIG. 3-13d

FIG. 3-13e

FIG. 3-13f

FIG. 3-13g

under, give the thread a gentle yank to pull out the corner and stitch (Fig. 3-12c). Do not try to fold the whole corner under before stitching it. Fold and stitch one edge under, anchor the corner and then stitch the next edge, as described above.

6. *Long sharp points* can be troublesome because you need to fold under a lot of fabric allowance into a small space. You will need to trim off as much of the allowance as you can without trimming too much, which can create raw threads. Begin by trimming off some of the tip of the point (Fig. 3-13a). Then fold and stitch under one edge up to the point. Place two stitches at the point to anchor it. Now this is tricky. Lift up the appliqué and reach under with your fine scissors and trim off a bit of the stitched edge (Fig. 3-13b). It is easier to stitch the edge under before trimming it. Then trim a bit off of the remaining edge, but not too much (Fig. 3-13c). Once the point is anchored, push the trimmed edge under using your fingers and needle until all the raw threads are hidden. Continue stitching the adjacent edge (Fig. 3-13d).

Another way to appliqué long sharp points is to make several folds in the corner seam allowance instead of trimming it. After stitching up to the point, fold the fabric under (Fig. 13-13e) and then fold it again (Fig. 3-13f). Finally, fold it on the fold line using your fingers and needle to push it under (Fig. 3-13g).

Moistening these corners helps them behave. Sometimes they do not always turn out as sharp as you expect. Try using both methods of trimming and folding, combining them to get the results you want. It takes practice and experimentation.

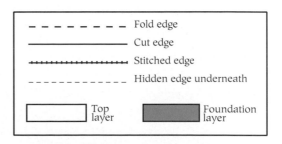

– – – – –	Fold edge
———	Cut edge
–+–+–+–	Stitched edge
- - - - -	Hidden edge underneath
☐	Top layer
▨	Foundation layer

KEY for figures shown on page 19-20.

7. To work the *inward corners*, first clip into the corner. Do not worry about not having enough edge to turn under. Students are often fearful about that. The corners will not turn under properly without clipping them right to the point (Fig. 3-14a). Fold and stitch the edge under to the corner (Fig. 3-14b). If necessary, add an extra stitch right at the point. Use your needle to tuck any loose threads under. Continue on the adjacent edge (Fig. 3-14c).

8. *Concave curves* must be clipped to enable them to fold under. A tighter curve will require more clips and a larger curve will need less. A very small circle needs clipping, but no removal of fabric. A larger circle will need some of the center removed to create an allowance of ⅛" (Fig. 3-15a).

Concave curves can be turned under in one swoop of the needle: after the curve is clipped, hold the edge down on the left with your left finger or thumb. Use the needle to turn the whole edge under in one motion (Fig. 3-15b). Fingerpress the edge to keep it under and then stitch it down (Fig. 3-15c). If you see that your curves look more angular than curved, cut more clips where needed to make a graceful curve.

9. Do not clip *convex curves*. Clipping convex curves can make unwanted points appear. Fold the edge under at one point (Fig. 3-16a). Make a stitch and refold the edge. Continue to fold and stitch around the curve (Fig. 3-16b). Sometimes you can make more than one stitch without refolding, depending on the degree of the curve. If a curve is not as smooth as you would like, use the tip of your needle to move the underneath allowance in or out to make it smooth.

10. To finish off the end of the thread, make a loop at the last stitch on the top. Bring the needle through the loop and pull it tightly (Fig. 3-17).

11. Bring the needle up and clip off the end of the thread. This will prevent knots on the back and keep the work neat (Fig. 3-18).

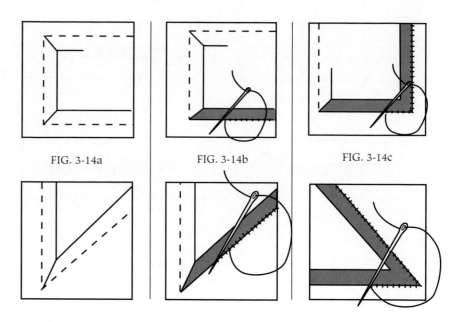

FIG. 3-14a   FIG. 3-14b   FIG. 3-14c

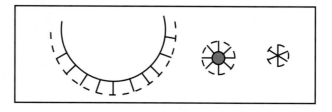

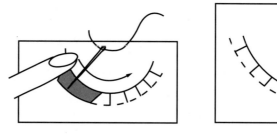

FIG. 3-15a

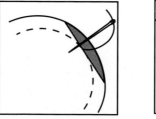   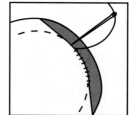

FIG. 3-15b   FIG. 3-15c

FIG. 3-16a   FIG. 3-16b

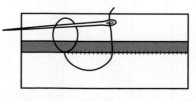   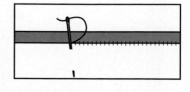

FIG. 3-17   FIG. 3-18

TROUBLE SHOOTING AND HELPFUL HINTS

■ Appliqué takes practice. Your skill will improve the more you do this work.

■ Be sure to clip into the inward corners clear to the point and use the tip of your needle to push in any raw edges. You may find the point a little more opened up than you would like, but that is inevitable. You'll find it won't be noticed in the overall look of the piece.

■ Outward corners take practice. It takes some experimentation to determine the best way to accomplish the effect you want. They may be more rounded than you want, but again they won't be noticed.

■ Fabric will draw up as you work so that when you come to a corner it may have shifted from its original position. You may have to compensate for this by folding the corner beyond its marked position to keep it where you want it. Sometimes I have stitched too close to the corner and there is not enough to turn under. The only way to fix this is to rip out the corner stitches and fold further back.

■ I usually tell students to allow at least ⅛" to fold under. If you are experienced, you may prefer to fold under less to create a finer piece of work with smaller detail. However, I suggest starting with ⅛".

■ I like to think of appliqué as shaping the fabric. Sometimes you must be aggressive with the corners, pushing and shoving edges under, moistening the fabric and even using a spot of glue on a pin tip to secure raw threads. Other times you can make a gentle curve with no effort.

■ I find that on different days my stitching varies with my working mood. Sometimes I make fine even stitches and other days my stitches are uneven. Sometimes I am in a hurry to finish a piece. Other times if my mind is occupied with a good program on television, I can sit by the hour doing good stitching as long as I don't get bored. However, watching television can be a liability if it demands constant attention such as dancing or sports. Some programs do not require constant watching. The radio, audio tapes or CDs are sometimes a better idea.

CHAPTER 4

CREATING FIGURES

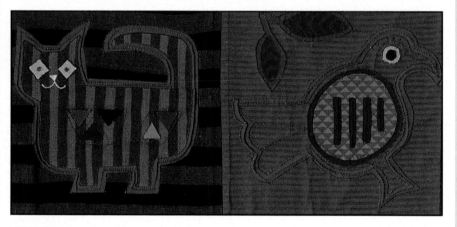

PHOTO 4-1

The first part of this chapter describes the use of channels, which are the building blocks of mola appliqué. Looking at the photos in this chapter will help you understand how molas are constructed. In the second part of this chapter you will learn how to make a simple block from the quilt, PRIMITIVE CRITTERS (page 27, detail above). You will learn to do channel appliqué, tandem appliqué, double appliqué, and various kinds of details.

CHANNELS

Creating a channel is the first step of making a traditional mola. The Kuna Indians use at least 12 variations of channels, from a single outline to seven-outline channels (Fig. 4-1). Notice the difference in these channels. There are several methods of achieving the three-, five- and seven-outline channels. The Kunas have many challenging ways of creating them with pieces and layers of fabric added, but I seldom use these complex methods and don't teach them.

If you have a chance to look at some molas, see if you can figure out how they were made. Remember that one layer is worked and then another is placed over it, cut, and stitched so that only a thin outline of the underneath layer is revealed. Most molas are built up from the foundation, rather than cut from the top down. This is self evident upon close scrutiny. Only two-color and a few three-color molas are made starting with the top layer being cut first.

FIG. 4-1

■ **PHOTO 4-1.**
Detail from the quilt, PRIMITIVE CRITTERS. The cat is one of a pair done as tandem appliqué with colorful triangles appliqued on top; the bird is done with channel appliqué with double appliqué details, explained in this chapter. (Full view page 27.)

■ **FIG. 4-1.**
Five basic kinds of channels.

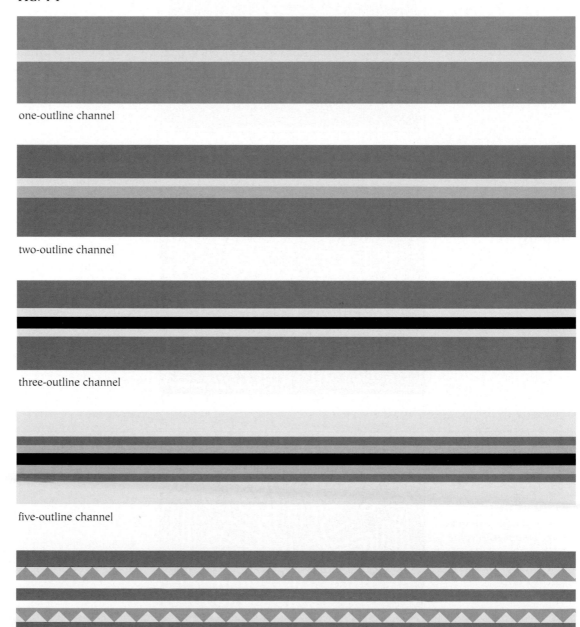

one-outline channel

two-outline channel

three-outline channel

five-outline channel

seven-outline channel with sawtooth edge

Single Channels

Photos 4-2 to 4-6 show examples of the following uses of single channels.

■ **PHOTO 4-2.**
Pig mola. Channel outline defines the main figure (the pig.)

PHOTO 4-2

■ In molas of many colors a channel usually outlines and defines the main figure. Notice the green outline around the pig (Photo 4-2). Green is the foundation layer showing through the outline cut in the top red layer.

■ **PHOTO 4-3.**
Nativity mola. Channel creates a format for the appliquéd figures.

PHOTO 4-3

■ A channel can create a framework for main figures which are appliquéd on top. In the Nativity mola (Photo 4-3), the yellow outline creates a stable for the infant, angels, and animals.

■ **PHOTO 4-4.**
Mirror image animal mola. Channels outline the animals and also fill in the background with maze-like detail.

PHOTO 4-4

■ Channels can be used to fill the space around a figure with maze-like designs, like the yellow lines around the animals in the black and yellow animal mola (Photo 4-4).

PHOTO 4-5

■ Channels can fill up the space inside of the figure as well as around it, covering the entire surface of the mola with maze-like detail as in the bird mola (Photo 4-5).

■ **PHOTO 4-5.**
Bird mola. The entire mola surface is created with channels, inside and around the figure.

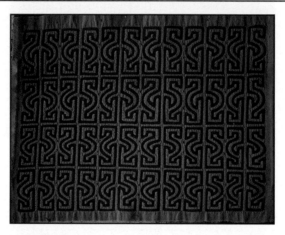

PHOTO 4-6

■ Channels can be designed in geometric shapes and repeated or combined with other repeats to form an overall pattern (Photo 4-6). This geometric mola is made with orange over a red foundation.

■ **PHOTO 4-6.**
Repeat pattern mola. The channel makes up a geometric repeat pattern.

Multiple Channels

Photos 4-7 to 4-10 show examples of the following uses of multiple channels.

PHOTO 4-7

■ The cross (Photo 4-7) is defined with a triple outline. Another frames the entire mola. This outline is made with three layers: red on the top, a middle layer of yellow, and a blue foundation. The figures are made up of appliqué over the top layer. The background is filled in with reverse appliqué slits made from several colored inserts under the top layer.

■ **PHOTO 4-7.**
Religious symbols mola. The cross is defined and the mola is framed with a triple channel.

■ **PHOTO 4-8.**
A channel of five outlines creates the format for the crucifixion.

PHOTO 4-8

■ The format of the crucifixion mola (Photo 4-8) is made of five outlines. There is an orange layer over a red layer over a chartreuse foundation. A narrow black center line was inlaid within the channel directly over the chartreuse foundation layer. The other details were made by cutting and removing parts of the orange top and replacing them with many colors appliquéd over the red middle layer (inlay appliqué). Each section was then topped with a matching black shape.

■ **PHOTO 4-9.**
Pig mola. A double outline channel outlines the pig.

PHOTO 4-9

■ Another pig mola (Photo 4-9) has two outlines made in an unexpected way. First the red pig was appliquéd over the orange foundation. The entire piece was covered with a black layer, cut and stitched with a channel to reveal a narrow outline of both the red appliqué and the orange foundation. Most of the other details are appliquéd on top with un-mola appliqué.

■ **PHOTO 4-10.**
Joined alligators mola. Seven outlines make up the channel defining the figures.

PHOTO 4-10

■ The joined alligators in Photo 4-10 feature a variation of the seven-outline channel, with two sawtooth edges. The outlines of some molas can become very complex. I seldom incorporate these more complex variations.

Hmong Appliqué

Another style of appliqué, done by Hmong women from Asia, uses channel appliqué and is similar in some ways to mola work. It is called "Pa ndau" (Photo 4-11). The main difference between molas and Pa ndau is that Pa ndau pieces are usually square with rigid design elements repeated and rotated around the center point and in each corner of the design. Some of these works are very fine, with very little seam allowance folded under. Like mola work, the Pa ndau technique is primarily composed of channels. Also, both have appliqué details over the top layer. Squares and diamonds are some-

PHOTO 4-11

times used in Pa ndau. Many color molas have a profusion of appliquéd details. Both Pa ndau and the more complex molas feature sawtooth edges in their designs. Both types of needlework also use embroidered details – French knots inside the channels and tiny triangles arranged in regu-

lar patterns on Pa ndau and embroidery as a fill-in method on molas.

USING PRIMITIVE CRITTERS PATTERNS

Patterns for the quilt, PRIMITIVE CRITTERS (below), are an easy introduction to mola figures. The various figures are made up with single channel appliqué, tandem appliqué, and double appliqué. In this quilt, I used fabrics that I silkscreened as well as commercial fabrics with fine geometric designs.

Outlining a Figure with
Single-Channel Appliqué

A channel is made by making a cut in the top layer and simply folding under and stitching the edges to the foundation layer underneath. Sometimes it will be a continuous line (Fig. 4-2) or it may be used to define a shape.

■ **PHOTO 4-11.**
Hmong Pa ndau work.

■ **PHOTO 4-12.**
PRIMITIVE CRITTERS, 43" x 42", 1993. (Details, page 22, 35).

■ **FIG. 4-2.**
Creating a single channel.

FIG. 4-2

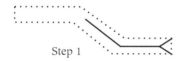
Step 1

Step 2

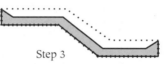
Step 3

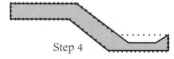
Step 4

1 D	2 A	3 E	4 A	5 B	6 D
7 E	8 F	9 C	10 C	11 E	12 B
13 A	14 E	15 F	16 F	17 D	18 E
19 D	20 F	21 E	22 C	23 A	24 F
25 A	26 B	27 F	28 A	29 B	30 E
31 C	32 D	33 B	34 D	35 C	36 F

Key to block patterns for
PRIMITIVE CRITTERS

PHOTO 4-12

To follow the instructions given below, (Fig. 4-3), use one of the patterns for the PRIMITIVE CRITTERS or draw your own shape. Keep it very simple. Note: the lines marked on the PRIMITIVE CRITTERS patterns are the *cutting* lines.

FIG. 4-3

Creating a single channel mola around a figure.

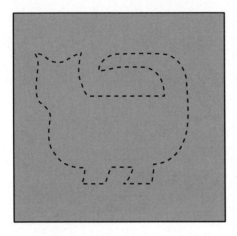

Step 1

1 Trace the design from the pattern to a 7½" square of fabric that will be the top layer, the dominant color. This size fabric allows for seaming and extra allowance for any drawing up that may occur.

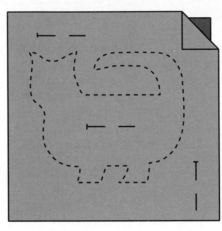

Step 2

2 Pin or baste the top layer to a contrasting underneath layer. The underneath layer must be larger than the size of the figure, but does not have to be as large as the top layer.

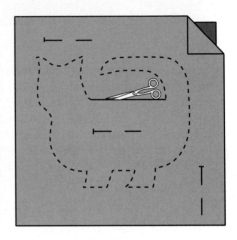

Step 3

3 Poke the tip of your scissors through the top layer on the traced line and cut about 2". Be careful to cut accurately on the line.

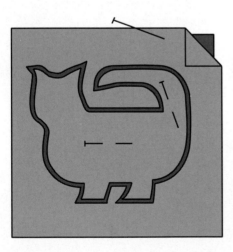

Step 6

6 Stitch until you are back to the starting place. Move the pins around as needed to hold loose pieces in place. Keep turning the work as necessary.

Step 7

7 Continue in the same way to sew the inner edge of the figure.

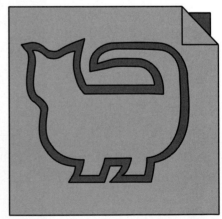

Step 8

8 As you work, try to keep the width of the channel even, about ¼".

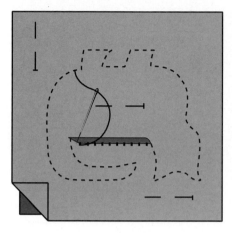

Step 4

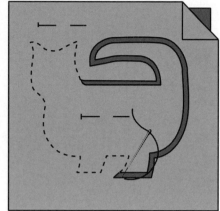

Step 5

4 Starting with the outer edge of the background around the figure, start folding the edge under with a seam allowance of about ⅛". Make tiny whip stitches, even in size and spacing, no farther apart than ⅛". Turn the work as needed to a comfortable position.

5 Follow the stitching instructions in Chapter 3 as you continue to sew the channel around the figure.

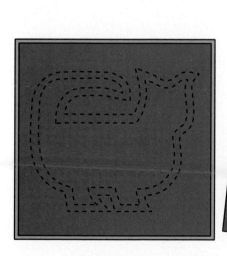

Step 9

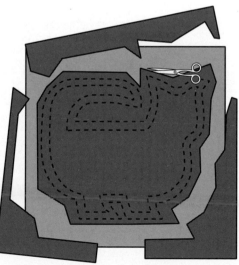

Step 10

9-10 You may want to turn the work over and trim away the extra fabric around the figure. This will make it less bulky for quilting. If you want to use it for seaming into a garment or a tote bag, you may want to keep the underlayer intact to give it body.

Tandem Appliqué

With tandem appliqué you can create two identical blocks with opposite color combinations. The Kunas use variations of this technique to create matching molas. If the design is an intricate maze, this method can be very challenging. For a simple design it is easy. To follow the instructions for tandem appliqué in Fig. 4-4, use the same block as in the previous exercise or another PRIMITIVE CRITTER pattern.

FIG. 4-4   **Creating tandem channel appliqué figures.**

Step 1

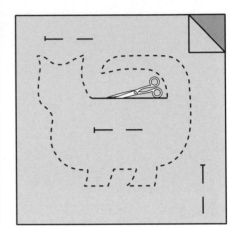

Step 2   Step 3

1 Trace the design from the pattern to a 7½" square of fabric that will be one top layer.

2 Pin or baste the marked fabric to a contrasting square of the same size that will be another top layer.

3 Poke the tip of your scissors through the two layers on the traced line and cut out the entire figure, being careful to cut right on the lines.

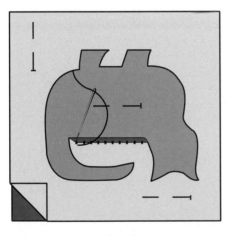

Step 6

Step 7   Step 8

6 Working on one mola at a time, start folding under and stitching the outer edge around the figure as explained in Fig. 4-3, Step 4.

7 Continue to sew around the figure.

8 Stitch back to your starting place.

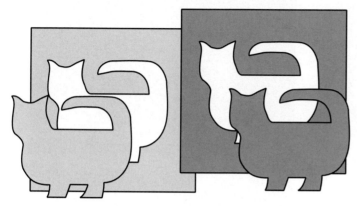

Step 4

4 This results in four pieces: two figures and two surrounding backgrounds.

Step 5

5 Exchange the figures so that they are surrounded by the contrasting color. Pin in place to two foundations of a third color.

Step 9

9 Repeat with the inner edge of the figure, revealing a channel between the two colors. Keep the channel an even width, about ¼".

Step 10

10 Repeat the stitching procedure with the second mola so that you have two squares with the figures and surrounding backgrounds of opposite colors. If you wish, turn the pieces over and trim away the excess fabric from the back.

Examples of tandem appliqué.

PHOTO 4-13

PHOTO 4-14

■ **PHOTO 4-14.**
KUNA ECHOES is a quilt that I made to use in a bedroom completely decorated with molas on all the walls. I wanted to make a quilt that would echo the molas without detracting from them. Notice the center blocks of the quilt feature animal figures made in tandem (Photo 4-15). I used black and coral for the figure blocks.

■ **PHOTO 4-13.**
I used tandem appliqué in the quilt, SKYLARK. It is made up of 16 blocks, which are eight pairs of blocks made in tandem. In some of the blocks, the design is reversed. I used a magenta foundation for four of the pairs and light blue for the other four pairs.

PHOTO 4-15

■ PHOTO 4-16.
I also used the tandem method to make the small quilt, I WISH I'D BEEN AN ANTHROPOLOGIST. I added quite a bit of channel detail within the figures, their surrounding backgrounds and the large faces. The channels suggest the painted faces of tribes from various regions in the world. Around the small figures, I wanted to suggest generic glyphs that might relate to aboriginal peoples anywhere.

PHOTO 4-16

Outlining a Figure with Double Appliqué

The Kuna Indians use double appliqué most of the time for adding details to figures. They also use it to create secondary figures or the main figure of a mola. I made some of the figures in PRIMITIVE CRITTERS this way. The steps in Fig. 4-5 illustrate outlining with double appliqué.

FIG. 4-5

Outlining a figure with a double channel appliqué.

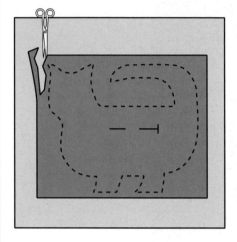

Step 1

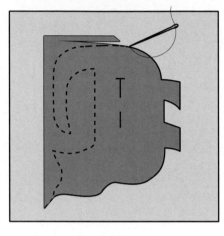

Step 2

Step 3

1 Trace the pattern to a small piece of fabric. Pin it over a foundation square measuring 7½". Starting at any point on the figure, start cutting ⅛" outside the pattern line.

Note: For this step of double appliqué, the dashed line indicates the fold line, not the cutting line as it usually does in the PRIMITIVE CRITTER patterns.

2 Cutting as you go, fold under and stitch the edge all around the figure.

3 Continue until you are back to the start. You now have an appliquéd figure.

Step 4

Step 5

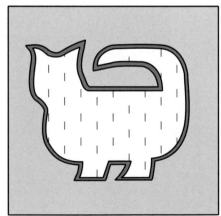

Step 6

4 Trace and cut another figure from a contrasting fabric. This time cut it out on the line or, just to be safe, a hairline beyond the line. Remember, appliqué can shrink, drawing up as you work, so cut generously. Pin this figure over the previously appliquéd figure.

5 Fold and stitch the edge under so that there is about ⅛" of the underneath appliquéd figure revealed all around it.

6 When you stitch back to the start, you now have a figure ready for the addition of whatever details you may like to try.

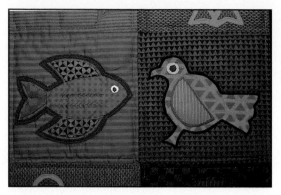

Photo 4-17

Photo 4-18

Details of PRIMITIVE CRITTERS. (Full quilt, page 27).

4-17. *Single appliqué detail on the tail and fins of the fish; double appliqué wing on the bird.*

4-18. *Single narrow appliqué strips; cut out dots on the turtle, slits on the bird.*

4-19. *Single appliqué circle with triangles cut through, double appliqué leaves with the bird; traditional feather shape appliqued to the duck with a double appliqué baby duck.*

4-20. *Slits on the cat with two colors; inlaid triangles on the duck.*

Photo 4-19

Photo 4-20

Details – Double Appliqué, Slits, Dots, Triangles, and Embroidery

There is no limit to the details you can add to figures. Although the Kuna molas are totally covered with detail, I take liberties with their tradition and add only as much as I want. In PRIMITIVE CRITTERS, I added only a few details, including eyes, to each figure – just enough to make it fun but not tedious.

You can put wings and feathers on birds, fins and scales on fish, or whatever shapes you desire. I used double appliqué and some single appliqué. Try geometric shapes – cut and stitch your own ideas or use some of the suggested shapes in Fig. 4-6.

Fig. 4-6

Fig. 4-6.
Double and single appliqué detail suggestions.

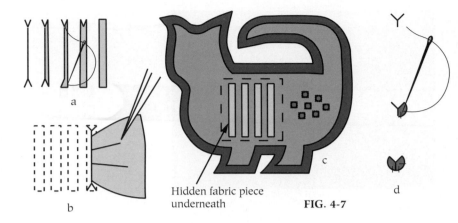

Hidden fabric piece underneath

FIG. 4-7

■ FIG. 4-7.
Creating slits and dots.

■ FIG. 4-8.
Creating triangles, cut out and inlaid.

■ FIG. 4-9.
Inlay and cut-through diamonds.

The Kunas use slits, triangles, and dots for fill-in details. The popular slits are cut and stitched as shown in Fig. 4-7a. Insert small pieces of fabric underneath groups of slits between the top and underlayer to add more color. It is a little tricky to add a color under the slits within a figure that is already stitched. To do so, cut a piece of fabric to fit a group of slits. Cut one slit. Insert the cut piece through the slit (Fig. 4-7b) and, using the point of your scissors, flatten it and position it in place (Fig. 4-7c).

The Kunas usually plan ahead and place their inserts in position before putting the top layer over the foundation, basting them in place so that the basting stitches make it obvious where the inserts have been placed. I prefer inserting the fabric pieces later so that I can decide afterwards on whether I want to use them and on their color placement.

The random dots (Fig. 4-7d) that Kunas add

to their molas are very challenging. To make a dot opening, cut a very small "Y" shape. Turn the edges under with the needle and stitch them down with tiny stitches. This is a very finicky detail that you may want to try or ignore.

There are two ways of working triangles (Fig. 4-8). For both methods, first cut and stitch ½" triangles through the top layer, revealing the layer beneath. One method is to inlay smaller appliquéd triangles within the ½" triangles. Another method, if you are working with three layers, is to cut and stitch a smaller triangle within each ½" triangle, revealing the underneath layer. Try these inlay and cut-through methods with other shapes such as diamonds (Fig. 4-9), circles or X's.

It is also a tradition of the Kuna molas to feature embroidery work. The embroidery is done with embroidery floss or with regular thread. Use running, chain, and fly stitches to embroider tiny details such as whiskers or other textures to create visual interest.

I used two mola type figures in the quilt, ISLAND FEVER (opposite). I made this quilt before I made my fifth visit to the San Blas Islands. During my visit, I had a nasty sore throat and cough. It was also very windy. Later the quilt reminded me of the white caps over the turbulent water and the hot shapes that I appliquéd over the center recalled how my irritated throat felt.

Notice the two figures in the quilt, the toucan and the cat. Both were made in the traditional Kuna way with channels defining them and then repeated around them. I used double appliqué to fill the space within the figures and the leaf.

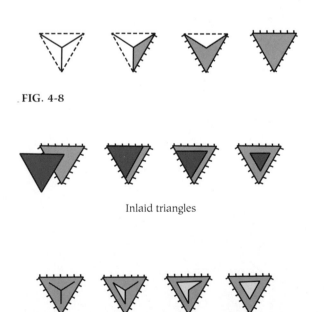

FIG. 4-8

Inlaid triangles

Cut-through triangles

FIG. 4-9

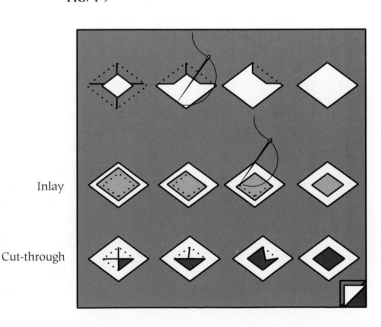

Inlay

Cut-through

PHOTO 4-21

■ **PHOTO 4-21**
ISLAND FEVER, 45" x 45", 1993. Toucan with double appliqué feathers, eye and leaf, single appliqué beak and feet, embroidery. Cat with double appliqué mid section and legs, single appliqué head, nose, mouth and tail, embroidery.

CHAPTER 5

CREATING MOTIFS

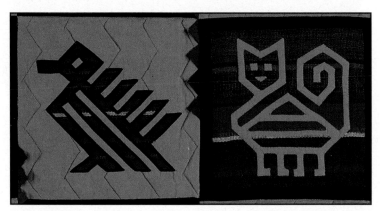

PHOTO 5-1

This chapter contains instructions for more mola techniques, illustrated by examples from Kuna molas and quilts I have made. You can use the patterns in this book for GUATEMALAN GLYPHS to try a figure with intersecting outlines and the techniques of un-mola appliqué and triple channel appliqué. Use the FLOWERS DECO patterns to learn inlay appliqué. Instructions are also given for making sawtooth borders.

Photos 5-2 and 5-3 show examples of the use of channels to create motifs. I made each block of the quilt, PLUS-X (right), with channels forming a "plus" sign echoed within a circle shape. I silkscreened striped "plus" sign motifs on fabric for the foundation layer and turned them 45 degrees to go under the dark blocks. I used the same silkscreened motifs with solid fabrics to create the alternating blocks.

EQUINOX (below) features a large sun motif made up mostly of channels. The center medallion has a dark brown layer over a foundation made up of strip-pieced yellows and oranges. I cut away most of the brown over the face to keep it warm and sunny. I then appliquéd the features over the face. I suggested the feeling of the sun rays in the strips around the center, using accents of channel appliqué and quilting.

I created the quilt, GUATEMALAN GLYPHS (page 41), using angular motifs from Guatemalan weavings, adapted to fit several of my favorite techniques. Although this quilt uses Kuna techniques, these types of motifs are not used in the Kuna culture. I used woven Guatemalan fabrics in this quilt. Because these fabrics are very coarsely woven and too heavy to fold under and manipulate, they could not be used for the upper appliqué layers. However, they worked well as foundation layers.

PHOTO 5-2

■ **PHOTO 5-1.**
Detail from the quilt, GUATEMALAN GLYPHS. The bird (Block 7) was done with a triple channel, explained in this chapter and the cat (Block 8) uses the un-mola appliqué. (Full view, page 41).

■ **PHOTO 5-2.**
PLUS-X, 41" x 48", 1990.

■ **PHOTO 5-3.**
EQUINOX, 50" x 49", 1987.

PHOTO 5-3

The brilliant color combinations of stripes in these Guatemalan fabrics and the motifs create an atmosphere of Guatemala. The highlands of this Central American country are saturated with colorful woven costumes worn by Indians of Mayan descent. Each village has its special weaving tradition.

USING GUATEMALAN GLYPHS PATTERNS

Note: the lines on the GUATEMALAN GLYPHS patterns are the *fold* lines, not the cutting lines.

Figure with Intersecting Outlines

Sometimes a channel crosses another channel, creating an intersection as in GUATEMALAN GLYPHS Pattern A (Block 2 on key, page 41). I have found students tend to want to stitch straight through an intersection, ignoring the corners, as shown in Fig. 5-1a. When you come to a place where two channels cross, you must continue around the edge of the channel, turning the corner as shown in Fig. 5-1b. Then appliqué the "between pieces" to the foundation layer of fabric.

Un-Mola Appliqué

To do the un-mola technique, try it on GUATEMALAN GLYPHS Pattern A. Cut ⅛" *outside of the pattern lines instead of down the center of the channel,* (Fig. 5-2, Step 1). Continue cutting and sewing as shown in Fig. 5-2, Step 2.

I used un-mola appliqué for some of the motifs in the quilt GUATEMALAN GLYPHS to show more of the striped Guatemala foundation fabric. With the un-mola technique, all the fabric surrounding the motif is removed, revealing a lot of the foundation fabric. With channel appliqué, only the striped foundation fabric shows through the channels.

FIG. 5-1

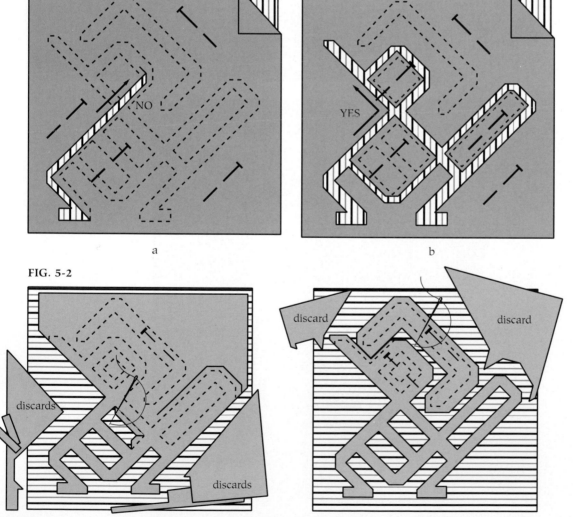

a   b

FIG. 5-2

Step 1   Step 2

■ **PHOTO 5-4.**
GUATEMALAN GLYPHS, 41" x 41", 1993.

■ **FIG. 5-1.**
Intersecting channels – wrong and right way.

■ **FIG. 5-2.**
Creating an un-mola motif.

PHOTO 5-4

1 C	2 A	3 B	4 E
5 D	6 E	7 F	8 C
9 E	10 G	11 F	12 B
13 G	14 D	15 C	16 A

Key to block patterns for
GUATEMALAN GLYPHS.

41

PHOTO 5-5

PHOTO 5-6

■ **PHOTO 5-5.**
Three Saws Mola by Marienela Tejeda. Triple channels define the saws.

■ **PHOTO 5-6.**
Mirror Bird Mola. Triple channels make up a format for the appliquéd figures.

■ **PHOTO 5-7.**
Eagle Mola. Triple channels fill in the background.

■ **PHOTO 5-8.**
Large Critter Mola. Triple channels fill in the figures and the background.

■ **PHOTO 5-9.**
Repeat Motif Mola. Triple channels make up the repeat pattern.

■ **FIG. 5-3.**
Creating the triple channel.

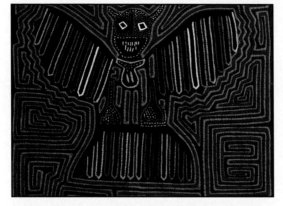

PHOTO 5-7

PHOTO 5-8

PHOTO 5-9

Triple Channel – Three-Layer Method

The three-outline channel is made by stacking three layers of fabric together. This is the one technique that comes close to the way mola making is usually described. The Kunas use triple channels in the same way single channels are used:

- To define a figure or motif (Photo 5-5);
- To create a frame for the figures (Photo 5-6);
- To fill space around a figure (Photo 5-7);
- To fill space inside and around a figure (Photo 5-8) and;
- To create repeat geometric designs (Photo 5-9).

To make a triple channel, the top layer is cut and stitched to form a wider channel – ½" in width is easily workable. To do this, it is necessary to cut and remove a narrow strip from the middle of the channel. Next, the revealed middle layer is slit and stitched to the foundation layer which is revealed inside the wider channel (Fig. 5-3).

FIG. 5-3

Step 1

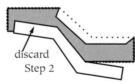

discard
Step 2

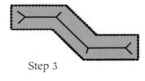

Step 3

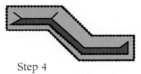

Step 4

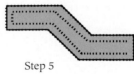

Step 5

PHOTO 5-10

■ **PHOTO 5-10.**
*SUNRISE SERENADE,
35" x 31", 1986. An ex-
ample of the triple chan-
nel technique.*

COLLECTION OF KATHY VARGA.

■ **PHOTO 5-11.**
*Detail of SUNRISE SER-
ENADE. To create four
sun motifs, I used the
triple channel method,
cutting the middle chan-
nel to reveal the bottom
layer.*

PHOTO 5-11

Use GUATEMALAN GLYPHS Pattern E, F, or G to follow the instructions below which are illustrated in Fig. 5-4.

FIG. 5-4   **Creating a triple channel motif.**

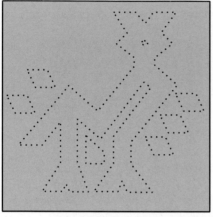

Step 1

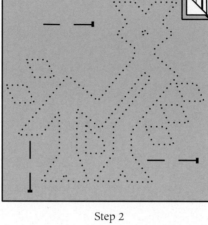

Step 2

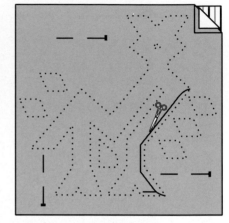

Step 3

1 Trace the design to a square of top layer fabric measuring 7½". *Trace the outer lines of the channel only. These are the fold lines for the top layer.* These patterns do not show a center cut line. Ignore the inner lines. They are drawn to show how the inner channel will look when the edges of the middle layer are turned under.

2 Pin or baste the marked top layer to two contrasting fabrics of the same size or a bit smaller, but larger than the motif. The middle layer will become the outline shown on the pattern as white. The bottom layer will become the inside wider channel shown as textured.

3 Poke the tip of your scissors through the channel. Start cutting so that the cut is about ⅛" inside the traced outer edge. *Do not cut on the traced line.*

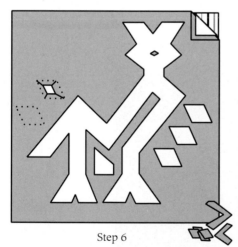

Step 6

Step 7

Step 8

6 Stitch back to your starting place. You now have an even channel ½" in width, revealing the middle layer. Trim away the extra allowance around the eye and appliqué the eye to the middle layer. This is a very tiny appliqué. Cut and stitch the small shapes around the figure.

7 Poke your scissors in the center of the channel through the middle layer, lifting the middle layer away from the bottom layer. Start cutting down the center of the channel, being careful not to cut the bottom layer. Cut as much as you wish because everything is already firmly stitched down and will not get out of position.

8 Fold the edge under and stitch it. Try to form an even outline of the middle layer about ⅛" in width.

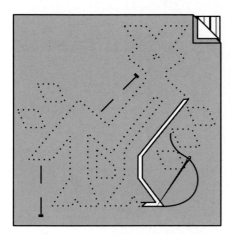

Step 4

discards   Step 5

4 Start folding the edge under on the traced line. Stitch the edge down. Keep cutting, folding, and stitching a few inches at a time, turning the work as needed and making even stitches.

5 Clip the edge at the inner corners to make them turn under and trim extra fabric at the outward corners. As you cut and stitch both sides of the channel, cut away the loose inner strips and discard them.

Step 9

Step 10

9 Continue in this way back to the start. You now have the figure outlined. The inner channel should be about ¼" in width. Stitch under the cut area around the eye.

10 Cut and stitch the other small openings around the figure.

FIG 5-5

FIG. 5-6

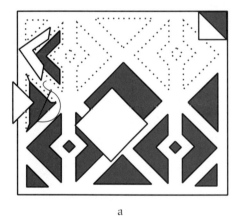

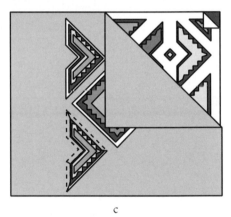

a   b   c

■ **FIG. 5-5.**
A geometric mola with the middle layer made up of inlay pieces.

■ **FIG. 5-6.**
Steps for inlay appliqué construction of Fig. 5-5.

INLAY APPLIQUÉ

Inlay appliqué is my term for a way the Kuna Indians use colored appliquéd shapes to interlock with each other like jigsaw puzzle pieces. This method is used most often in multi-color geometric designs.

Fig. 5-5 shows a mola design using inlay appliqué. This design was adapted from a complicated traditional mola (Photo 5-12) which covers a footstool, styled by Anne Wenzel of Panama City. It is made by placing a layer over the foundation which is cut and stitched with many angular openings to form a framework (Fig. 5-6a). These cutaway pieces are then replaced with matching shapes of many colors, inlaid within each opening (Fig. 5-6b). This design features inlays with sawtooth edges, a painstaking

Kuna touch which I use sparingly. Channels form in between the framework and the inlaid pieces, revealing the foundation.

The Kuna discipline would demand a third layer be placed over these appliquéd pieces (Fig. 5-6c), which would be cut by feeling the underneath appliqué edges. Smaller shapes of the top layer fabric would then be stitched over each inlaid shape. Slits would be made in the larger center diamond. I omit this third layer and enjoy doing the first stage of the inlay appliqué.

I have adapted this inlay method to non-geometric designs. The folk art figures and flowers in Photo 5-13 are inlaid within the gold top layer, over a plum foundation. The tulips used in the pillow shown in Photo 5-14 are also inlay appliqué within the black top layer, over a tan foundation.

Examples of inlay appliqué.

PHOTO 5-12

■ **PHOTO 5-12.**
Footstool with mola covering, styled and owned by Anne Wenzel.

■ **PHOTO 5-13.**
Folk art twins, made with inlay appliqué.

■ **PHOTO 5-14.**
Pillow with tulip design made with inlay appliqué.

PHOTO 5-13

PHOTO 5-14

USING FLOWERS DECO PATTERNS

To do the inlay appliqué in FLOWERS DECO (opposite), cut away the marked pieces of the top layer and stitch the cut edges of the top layer to the foundation. This forms the framework for pieces which will be inlaid, replacing the cutaway parts. This technique is a bit challenging, but give it a try. You may like it.

The inlay flower motifs in FLOWERS DECO were inspired by the designs of Charles Rennie Mackintosh, a textile designer from the early part of this century. The instructions below for the FLOWERS DECO patterns are illustrated in Fig. 5-7. Note: the lines on the FLOWERS DECO patterns are the *cutting* lines.

Creating a triple channel motif.

FIG. 5-7

Step 1

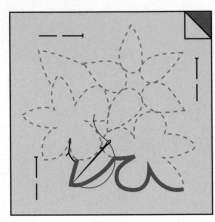

Step 2

1 Trace the pattern to a piece of top layer fabric measuring 10" square or 10" x 11½", whichever size fits the pattern you are using.

2 Pin this marked top layer to a foundation of the same size or a bit smaller. Start cutting *on the heavy line* and stitch around the outer edge, folding under a ⅛" seam allowance.

Step 3

Step 4

3 Stitch this way, cutting as you work, so that the entire edge around the design is stitched down to the foundation. This outer edge is the framework for the pieces which will be cut and inlaid. Remove the flowers and leaf shapes as a whole piece. Cut this piece apart on the lines to cut the flowers apart.

4 Use these cut pieces as templates to cut pieces in new colors. Pin the template pieces to the new fabric and cut the pieces to match exactly. This way you know that they will fit together. This method is more accurate than tracing from the pattern directly to each fabric.

PHOTO 5-15

Step 5

Step 6

Step 7

5 Inlay the new flowers and leaf shapes inside the framework. If there are several pieces of the same color such as the five separate petals of the same flower, cut the flower as one piece. When you stitch it, cut it apart as you work. Cut and sew the tiny detail pieces after the larger ones are in place. Position the flower and leaf pieces within the framework and pin or baste.

6 Turning under the edges ⅛", stitch down each piece, trying to make the channels in between the pieces even in width. If you find a piece coming out too small to keep the channel even, rip it out, cut a new one and do it over. Cut, place, and appliqué the flower centers after the petals are sewn in place.

7 In some designs there are tiny spaces between the flowers which should be the same color as the surrounding framework. If they are too tiny to be workable as appliqué pieces, embroider the tiny spaces using a satin stitch with thread that matches the framework.

■ **FIG. 5-8.**
The sawtooth edge.

SAWTOOTH EDGE USED BY KUNAS

If you would like to try the sawtooth edge (Fig. 5-8), this is how it is done. Cut the edge of the appliqué with slits. Fold under each corner of the slit and stitch it down. The Kunas keep the slits about ¼" apart. I make mine a bit farther apart. This sawtooth is not really as difficult as it looks, but it is time consuming.

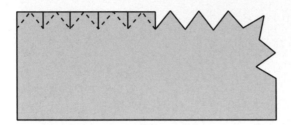

FIG. 5-8

VARIATIONS IN CREATING MOLA MOTIFS

Study the various techniques used in the motifs in the quilt, AFRICANA (opposite). The zebra, bird, and antelope were taken from a book published by Dover, *African Designs from Traditional Sources* by Geoffrey Williams.

The zebra is defined by the ends of the channels. The widths of the channels and the spaces between them vary, unlike most molas which have even channels and spaces. The antelope is a simple cutaway through the teal layer to the gold layer, enhanced with burgundy zigzag appliqué. The lizard (bottom left) is a network of channels, the gold layer cut through to the burgundy layer, which extend under the edge of the figure. A top layer of teal was cut away to define the edge of the lizard. The bird is defined by the cutaway edge of teal and by a burgundy channel inlaid within the teal opening.

The large mask (bottom right) is made up of inlay appliqué with all the pieces carefully cut so that a channel forms an even outline over the whole mask. The channel outlining the snake changes color because the underlayer was pieced of red and teal. Gold pieces are appliquéd over the snake with small dots as accents.

PHOTO 5-16

PHOTO 5-17

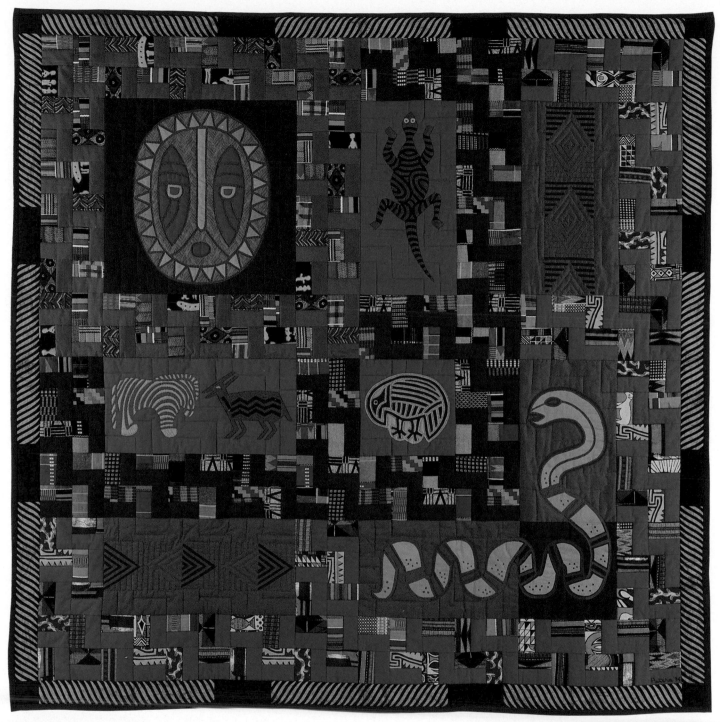

PHOTO 5-18

■ **PHOTO 5-18.**
AFRICANA, 64" x 64", 1994.

■ **PHOTO 5-16.**
Detail of AFRICANA. Lizard is a network of channels, the gold layer cut through to the burgundy layer.

■ **PHOTO 5-17.**
Detail of AFRICANA. Mask is made up of inlay appliqué cut so that channels form an uneven outline.

CHAPTER 6

CREATING GEOMETRIC REPEAT PATTERNS

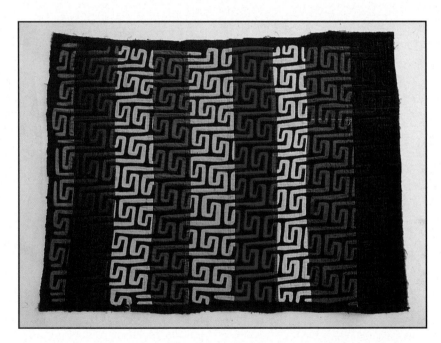

PHOTO 6-1

One of my favorite types of molas is the geometric repeat pattern. This chapter includes many examples of traditional and contemporary molas made with geometric repeat patterns. There are also instructions for the one- and three-outline geometric repeat patterns given in this book.

I am dazzled by the precision that the Kuna Indians are able to achieve. I have never been fortunate enough to watch one of these molas being designed and I don't know how the Indians can be so accurate without drafting skills or at least graph paper. One time a Kuna friend watched me drawing a design in my notebook on graph paper. She asked me if I could do one on fabric for her. I told her I would have to do it at home with my drafting and tracing equipment and send it to her. I could not do it freehand on the fabric on the spot as these bright Indian women do. Before using a computer, I used graph paper to design original molas or to copy intricate designs from Kuna molas. Today, part of the fun is drafting them on a computer, a time saver. (See Chapter 8 for tips on designing.)

There are so many variations in mola techniques and using strip piecing is one of my favorites. I first discovered this clever idea used by a Kuna woman on a mola I found in a local shop (Photo 6-1). She had used an underlayer made up of pieced strips. I wondered how she got the idea. It may have been for reasons of thrift or lack of enough fabric or it may have been an artistic decision. It set me off in many directions in my work.

The geometric repeat designs in this chapter are worked with two or sometimes three layers of fabric. The first time I tried this technique for a quilt, I was inspired by the strip-pieced mola in Photo 6-1. To make the quilt IN THE MOOD (below), I started with a square foundation layer which I pieced from eight strips. I used dark red over it, cutting and stitching the pattern so that the eight colors show through the intricate design. When I finished, I was in the mood to do more, so I used smaller squares in each color of the strips as the top layers over dark red underlayers. I chose a block arrangement which is similar to star quilt design. I worked on the center square while I was visiting the San Blas Islands and several of the Indians added some stitches to it.

■ **PHOTO 6-1.**
Geometric mola with strip pieced underlayer.

■ **PHOTO 6-2.**
IN THE MOOD, 44" x 44", 1984.

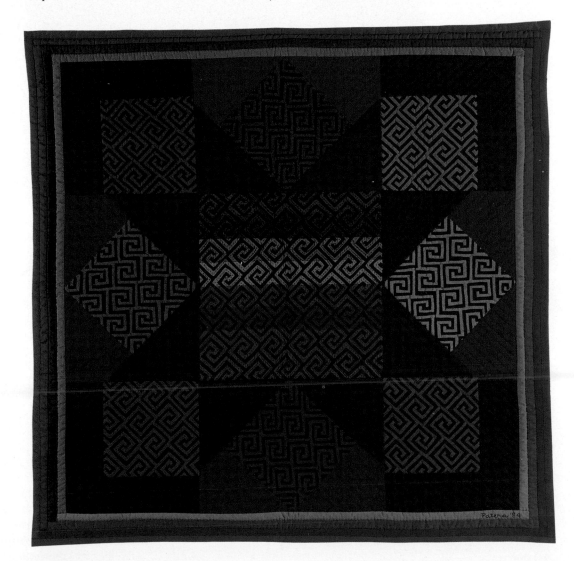

PHOTO 6-2

■ **PHOTO 6-3.**
PERFIDIA, 40" x 40",
1986.

■ **PHOTO 6-4.**
Mola blouse with tradi-
tional Kuna repeat pat-
tern. Adaptation of the
pattern used on a
bleached denim bag.

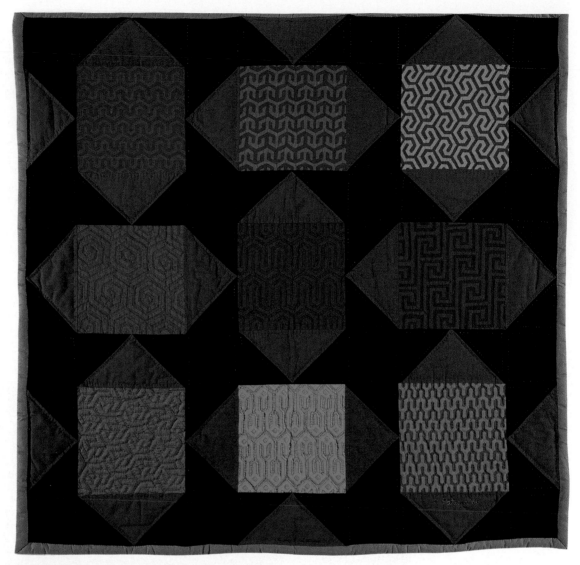

PHOTO 6-3

PHOTO 6-4

I then discovered the book, *Geometric Pat-*
terns and Borders, by David Wade, which is one
of my favorites. Designs from that book inspired
many ideas including my quilt, PERFIDIA
(above). Some of the geometric repeat patterns
used in PERFIDA are given on pages 98-100.

If you would like to try geometric repeat
designs, it is necessary to be very accurate, keep-
ing the channels and the spaces between channels an even width. If a quilt of these designs
seems overwhelming, try making a small piece
for a pillow or a bag similar to the one I made of
bleached denim and chambray (left) or use it for
a block of a quilt.

Photo 6-4 shows a mola blouse made with a
traditional geometric repeat Kuna design I have
always found appealing. I like it so much that I
have adapted it to simple versions with two and
three layers – Geometric Repeat Pattern A. Note:
the lines on the geometric repeat patterns are the
fold lines, not the *cutting* lines.

FIG. 6-1

GEOMETRIC REPEAT – ONE-OUTLINE PATTERNS (A-H)

Follow the instructions illustrated below to make the single outline version of Pattern A.

Step 1

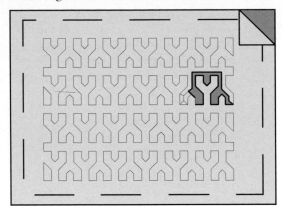

Step 2

1 Trace the design to a top layer of fabric measuring 7½" x 9½". Keep the design centered.

2 Pin or baste this marked top layer to a lower layer of the same size. Start on the outside edge (starting in the center can be very confusing). *Cut and stitch the edges under. Cut in the center of the channels, not on the fold lines.*

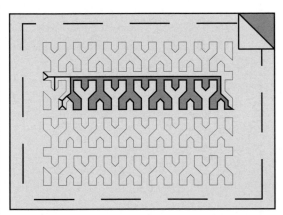

Step 3

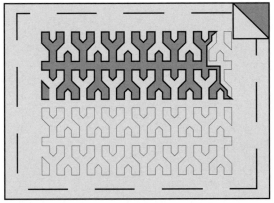

Step 4

3 Continue on in the same way. If using pins, keep moving them around to hold loose parts.

4 Keep cutting and stitching until you complete one set of the continuous pattern.

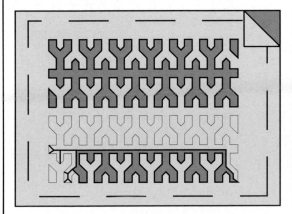

Step 5

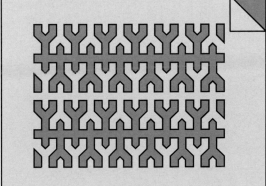

Step 6

5 Repeat to complete the other geometric repeats.

6 The design is now ready for setting into a dress, vest, or any other thing you may devise.

EXTENDING THE SIZE OF A GEOMETRIC REPEAT DESIGN

The patterns in this book are continuous repeats, meaning that you can make the pattern cover any size area you wish by repeating the pattern and cutting off the channels at the edge of the fabric. If you want the design to cover a larger area than the pattern size, trace the pattern once, line up the pattern with the previously traced lines and trace it again without a break in the pattern. The Geometric Repeat Patterns B, E, and F require a little shifting to enlarge in this manner. Move the pattern over the edge of the traced design until it matches up. A continuous version of Pattern A which covers a larger area is given on page 96.

You can make the design cover a smaller area by simply cutting off the design where you

Creating a geometric repeat with a triple channel.

FIG. 6-2

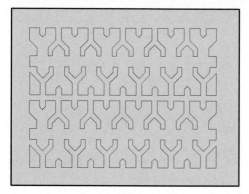

Step 1

1 Trace the outer edges of the pattern, ignoring the inside lines, to a top layer of fabric measuring 9" x 12". Keep the design centered.

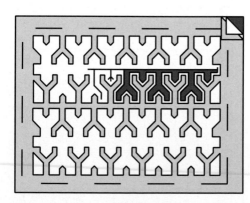

Step 4

4 Start cutting inside the center of the channels through the middle layer of fabric, being careful not to cut the foundation. Turn the edges under ⅛" and stitch to form an even outline of the middle layer, ⅛" wide.

want it to end. Some geometric repeat designs can also be used for borders by using only one of the continuous sets.

GEOMETRIC REPEAT – THREE-OUTLINE PATTERNS (A, I-J)

Students sometimes ask if a pattern for a one-outline design can be used for a three-outline design. The pattern cannot be used as is, but it can be specially adjusted for the addition of another outline.

Three layers are used to make a triple outline. This is the one time to follow the stacked layer approach. In this case, it is practical because the three colors are used over the entire surface.

Follow the instructions illustrated in Fig. 6-2 to make the triple-outline version of Pattern A.

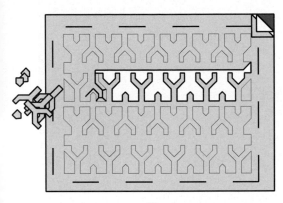

Step 2

2 Baste this marked top layer to two fabrics of the same size in contrasting colors. The middle layer will be the outer edge of the design shown on the pattern as white. The bottom layer is shown on the pattern as shaded.
Start cutting ⅛" *inside of the traced line*, using the inside line on the pattern as a guideline. Turn the edge under and stitch it. Discard the small pieces that are cut away as you work.

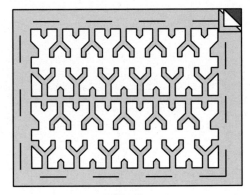

Step 3

3 Continue all the way around all of the channels. If pinning, keep moving your pins around as needed to hold loose cut parts. These channels should measure ½" in width and be ¼" apart. Turn the edge under and stitch it. Discard the small pieces that are cut away as you work.

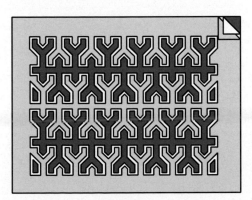

Step 5

5 Continue until completed. You now have a panel to use in any way you wish.

■ **PHOTO 6-5.**
MY OWN LITTLE WORLD, 61" x 61", 1990.

INNOVATIONS USING GEOMETRIC REPEATS

The quilts in Photos 6-5 to 6-11 all use geometric patterns in innovative ways. I made the quilt, MY OWN LITTLE WORLD (below), using some of the geometric repeat patterns in this book. At the time I enjoyed silkscreening my fabrics with small geometric designs, stripes, dots, and checkerboards in colors not available in stores. I used my favorite geometric repeat patterns with striped and lined fabrics to make nine different squares. I used the stripes in opposition to each other – horizontally for one layer and vertically for the other layer to achieve optical effects. For four of the blocks, I used three layers with a solid color for the middle layer.

I made SHADES OF MITLA (opposite) after visiting the site of the Zapotec Indian ruins at Mitla near Oaxaca, Mexico. When I looked at these wonderful stone mosaics (opposite, right), I was thrilled and knew they would adapt well to my favorite mola techniques. I studied my photographs and worked the designs out on the computer. That was fun in itself.

Then I started making the panels. The

PHOTO 6-5

underlayers of the top and center strips of the quilt were each pieced from two colors of fabric. A year after my visit I completed the quilted hanging. I tried to mimic the framing of the actual stone mosaics. The pyramid effects were done with strip piecing to suggest a feeling of Mexican pyramids.

Innovations using geometric repeats can be inspired by geometric patterns on artwork and on fabrics. Sometimes travel can introduce new ideas. I am still using these designs to make future Mitla wall hanging variations. Other times fabrics will suggest ideas for forming channels into new designs, either ordered or random.

There are so many unexplored ideas.

Some printed fabrics can be interpreted as checks or divided into squares. Take another look at my quilt, ISLAND FEVER (page 37). The square in the center was made with a Hoffman fabric printed with an interwoven pattern. I saw the fabric as a series of lined squares and worked my channel design through it, following the printed design. The upper left and lower right blocks of this quilt are also geometric repeat interpretations. I used two Hoffman fabrics printed with squares forming the traditional quilt pattern, Trip Around the World. Again, I followed the squares to make my channels,

■ **PHOTO 6-6.**
SHADES OF MILTA,
33" x 44", 1992.

■ **PHOTOS 6-7 and 6-8.**
Stone mosaics at the Zapotec Indian ruins at Mitla, Oaxaca, Mexico.

PHOTO 6-6

PHOTO 6-7

PHOTO 6-8

■ **PHOTO 6-9.**
RED, HOT AND BLUE,
59" x 60", 1991.

resulting in a camouflaged version of this fabric.

I made the quilt RED, HOT AND BLUE (below) in 1991, the year of the 100th birthday of Cole Porter and named it after one of his early musical comedies. I designed a simple motif and worked it into checkerboard printed fabrics of various scales. I wanted to see how many versions I could make by fitting the design into different sizes of checks. To work the design, I counted the squares of the checks the way you would for counted cross stitch (Fig. 6-3).

For the block shown in Photo 6-10, I printed

green checks on pink and turquoise fabrics and seamed them to make the top layer, carefully aligning the checks. I then worked the design through the squares. After that, I tried the design on a finer scale of checkerboard fabric (Photo 6-11). This time I seamed together orange and red for the underlayer and worked the design using four smaller checks together as one counted square. I also tried this on a very large checkerboard, dividing the large checks into fourths and visualizing them as one square. This is a bit tricky to do because you need to imagine the invisible square divisions.

PHOTO 6-9

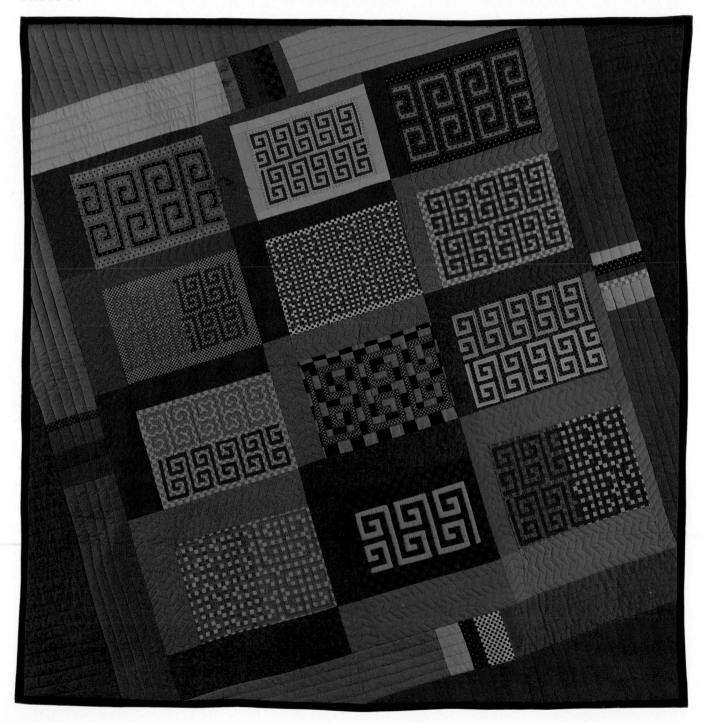

I tried other variations using dots instead of checks for some of the panels, counting the dots as squares (Fig. 6-4). Some dotted fabrics are printed with dots in orderly rows and others are printed with the dots spaced differently. Figure 6-4 shows how to handle two different dot configurations. Dots are not as well defined as squares so this too gets a little tricky.

The panels in the two upper corners of RED, HOT AND BLUE are done as tandem appliqué. To do the tandem appliqué, I placed the two dotted fabrics one over the other, carefully lining up the dots. Then I precut the entire design, following the position of the dots so that I could counter-exchange the two dotted fabrics over the red and orange foundations. This is an idea only for those who have mastered the simpler designs and who, like myself, like to keep exploring new ideas.

■ **PHOTOS 6-10 and 6-11.** *Details of RED, HOT AND BLUE.*

6-10. *Two silkscreened checkerboard fabrics seamed on top, red underlayer.*

6-11. *Two solid fabrics seamed for the underlayer, checkerboard on top layer.*

■ **FIG. 6-3.** *Several ways to work a geometric motif on checkerboard fabrics.*

■ **FIG. 6-4.** *Working the same motif on dotted fabrics.*

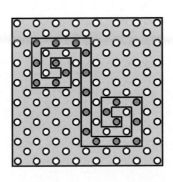

PHOTO 6-10

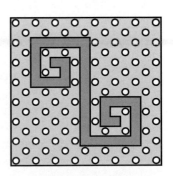

PHOTO 6-11

FIG. 6-3

▩ one check = one counted square ▦ four checks = one counted square

FIG. 6-4

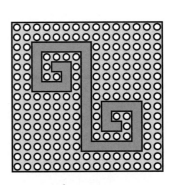

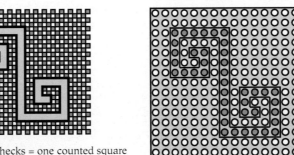

◧ one dot = one counted square

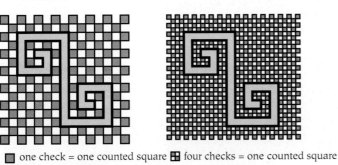

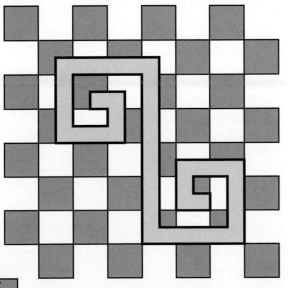

one dot = one counted square
▣ One space between dots also equals one counted square.

■ one fourth of a check = one counted square

61

CHAPTER 7

INNOVATIVE DEPARTURES

PHOTO 7-1

The best thing I have discovered in studying mola making is the treasure of new ideas molas inspire. Although I love to do some of the traditional Kuna designs, I also love to adapt their techniques to generate new concepts for contemporary quilts.

The purpose of this chapter is to help art quilt makers find new ideas. I usually begin my quilts by making a few experimental blocks, with no idea of how or if I will use them. If I like the blocks, then I must find some way to organize them into a design and then decide how many more I will need to complete a piece of work. I may repeat the same idea with variations or try other designs to add to the completed blocks.

PHOTO 7-2

■ **PHOTOS 7-1 (detail) and 7-2.**

HOCUS POCUS, 34" x 52", 1991. I used the same geometric appliqué design with many variations. I tried mixing stripes horizontally and vertically. Detail shows a solid red fabric stitched over a horizontally striped fabric. This quilt was juried into Quilt National '93 in Athens, Ohio.

SERIES BLOCKS

Some quilters make quilts in a series because when they are working on one idea, a variation of the same concept motivates them to try another quilt. I find this happening to me with blocks. When working on one block, another variation enters my head and I must try it.

In HOCUS POCUS (page 63) I used the same geometric appliqué design with many variations. I tried using stripes horizontally and vertically. I mixed stripes with solid fabrics (Figs. 7-1a and 7-1b). I also tried a new idea on several of the blocks, placing an appliqué circle directly over the foundation and then working the design so the circle is revealed through the channels (Fig. 7-1c).

On another block I pieced together three different colors for the underlayer, making each set of vertical designs a different color (Fig. 7-1d). On another block I worked each horizontal set of repeats with different underlayers (Fig. 7-1e). I positioned each color underneath one at a time,

carefully trimming away the excess fabric from the back when completed, so that the colored fabric previously worked would not be in the way of the next color. So many other ideas could also be used – multiple circles or triangles, in stripes, checks, and prints of all kinds (Figs. 7-1f).

In EXPERIMENT 1-2-3 (below) for the center panel I used yellow squares between rust and green striped fabrics, arranged at angles. I stitched the squares to the green striped fabric, traced the geometric design of channels to rust fabric, and worked it so that the yellow squares showed through. You will notice another experiment. Since the parts of the upper layer design were not connected as they are in many of the patterns, I omitted parts of the design. I then designed a piecing pattern for the outer sections of the quilt to echo the feeling of the appliqué design. To further tie in the piecing with the appliqué center, I appliquéd yellow squares to the surrounding piecing.

■ **FIG. 7-1.**
Variations in a series of blocks of the same pattern.

■ **PHOTO 7-3.**
EXPERIMENT 1-2-3, 36" x 36", 1992.

PHOTO 7-3

64

FIG. 7-1

■ **PHOTO 7-4.**
STUMBLING BLOCKS,
48" x 41", 1992. This
quilt was juried into
Diversity! (1995) at
Arrowmont, Gatlinburg,
Tennessee, sponsored by
the Studio Art Quilt
Association.

INCORPORATING A TRADITIONAL QUILT PATTERN

I decided it would be interesting to try combining the geometric repeat Pattern G, which resembles cubes, with the traditional quilt pattern, Tumbling Blocks. The result was the quilt, STUMBLING BLOCKS (below). To form the top layers, I traced one cube of the pattern onto separate fabrics cut into hexagons. I then combined three isometric diamonds in warm colors to form the underneath hexagonal layers. I worked each hexagon separately, placing the pieced hexagons under the traced cube hexagons. I then pieced the appliquéd hexagons together following my preplanned layout with the colors gradated from light to dark. I added some hexagons with black and white upper layers to give stronger contrast and more visual interest to the piece. I decided these clumps of black and white hexagons would represent the stumbling blocks in life that we all have to work through at times.

PHOTO 7-4

PHOTO 7-5

■ **PHOTO 7-5.**
CHAR'S CHARM QUILT,
48" x 51", 1988.

■ **FIG. 7-2.**
Drawing concentric arcs
with a compass.

CIRCLES AND ARCS

I have always been fond of using circles and parts of circles. For several of my quilts I drafted a pattern of concentric arcs. I placed a compass point at one corner of a square and drew arcs with the radii 1" apart (Fig. 7-2). When I trace this pattern to fabric, I may trace only some of the arcs at random or sometimes all of them. I then use these traced arcs to work channels over a foundation square. Usually these quilts are unplanned and I make as many blocks as I want to complete a quilt top.

In CHAR'S CHARM QUILT (above), I used fabrics that I had learned to silkscreen in a class by Katie Pasquini-Masopust. I combined them with several fabrics silkscreened by Katie plus some commercial fabrics. I used a gold solid fab-

ric under each square that was revealed when I cut and stitched the arcs. I also cut and stitched small circles in random squares. I then tried many arrangements of the squares until I decided on the final one. I call this a charm quilt because I did not repeat any fabrics.

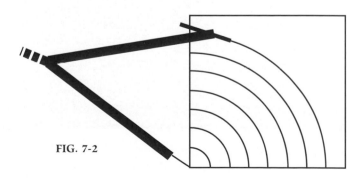

FIG. 7-2

■ **PHOTO 7-6.**
*RIPPLES, 45" x 45",
1989.*

That quilt triggered the idea of using large concentric circles to give the feeling of a pebble being thrown into calm water and sending out ripples. This time I silkscreened patterns of greens and blues on blue and turquoise fabrics of varying shades. Using a beam compass, I drew circles on a large sheet of paper, again making them 1" apart. I cut this sheet into squares and numbered them to keep them in the correct order. I arranged the fabric squares so they would be light in the center and darker at the edges and then traced the arcs from the pattern squares onto the fabrics. The quilt, RIPPLES (below), is the result.

LET THE FABRIC SPEAK TO YOU

It is always fun to try different fabrics together to work out a new channel appliqué design. I was inspired to make the quilt in Photo 7-7 after I found some wonderful streaked fabric by Hoffman. At the same time I found an idea for a radiant design. I traced the design to half of the Hoffman fabric and then placed it over the other half. The colors contrasted well enough so that

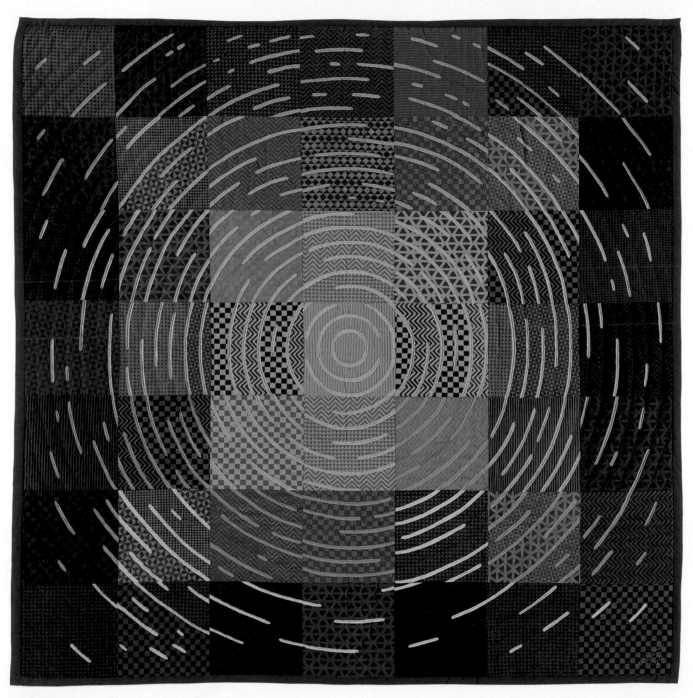

PHOTO 7-6

when it was worked, they defined the glowing design.

When I finished the panel, I had to decide what to do with it. Some concepts are good, but it is a challenge to decide what to do with them. I decided to keep the final piece a small work so that the panel would be emphasized. I chose browns for the border, gradating the shades slightly, so they would not intrude on the strong color of the panel. I sewed channels of varying angles and colors in the brown squares. When I completed that much, I thought the panel of col-

ors needed something in the center to give it meaning. But what? I finally decided on a simple curved figure that would project a feeling of accomplishment, of having gotten over an obstacle, or a spiritual feeling of RENEWAL, which is what I named it.

I reluctantly made HOT AND COOL RUNNINGS (page 70) as a fabric challenge. The challenge was to use the Gutcheon fabric, "Tenements." I did not feel motivated by this fabric and I usually stay away from challenges. At the same time, I had just discovered the work

■ **PHOTO 7-7.**
RENEWAL, 29" x 37", 1993.

PHOTO 7-7

69

■ **PHOTO 7-8.**
HOT AND COOL RUN-
NINGS, 28" x 33", 1994.

of the artist, Keith Haring. I made a simple design using my favorite tandem appliqué trick to create two panels, borrowing a Keith Haring approach, but I did not like the result. One of the panels did not work in the colors I had chosen with this fabric. I then cut up the offending panel, still wanting to use the figures that I had spent so much time creating. I appliquéd the

passable figures to fabric which I added to make the piece a respectable size. I then added the Haring-like graffiti, one of his characteristic trademarks. This was the part I liked best. I reworked the figures by adding more appliqué, determined to give the piece a theme of "street smarts" – rap music, hip hop, break dancing and graffiti.

PHOTO 7-8

PHOTO 7-9

THE CONTEMPORARY WORK OF HERTA PULS

A friend of mine from Wales, Herta Puls, has a way of using mola techniques in her own style to create contemporary designs. Herta and her husband, Oscar visit the San Blas Islands regularly and we have mutual friends in Panama City and on the islands. She is known around the United Kingdom and Europe and elsewhere for her teaching, writing, and making of molas and mola-influenced fiber art.

A master of innovative departures, Herta has a unique style of interpreting her subjects. A-Z (above) is a quilt she made for a grandchild. I looked at this piece several times before I understood that it was the alphabet. I was very fond of it before I came to that realization and when I discovered the letters, I loved it even more. The Kuna Indians often use lettering in their molas as pure design in a way that does not always make sense since they have no written language and don't always understand the positioning of letters.

Herta was inspired to do A-Z with pure lettering as the abstract design. She forms the letters in an unexpected, distorted, but flowing way that is very pleasing and unique. She alternated the sequence of the colors of the letters of each section. Each magenta letter is surrounded by red and each red letter is surrounded by magenta. In places she appliquéd the edges, varying the widths of the black channels between the letters. Notice how she left the opening in the letter "P" solid black. It gives the whole work a needed focal point like a bull's eye. She then topped off the quilt with a layer of gray, cut and stitched to cover up the "joins" between each letter.

Herta used a similar technique but with more colors for the quilt, LET'S PLANT A TREE (page 73). This time, she used a print fabric for the foundation under the entire piece. Notice how its exposure adds a sparkle to the main edges of the tree where it is revealed to form a glowing outline. Her intention was to show how a new tree could be planted where an old tree had been burned out, showing the new growth

■ **PHOTO 7-9.**
A-Z, 53" x 71", Herta Puls, 1976.
PHOTO: MICHAEL WICKS

contrasted with the burned remains of the original tree. Later she found a quotation by Johann Wolfgang Goethe that expressed her original meaning: "If the world shall end tomorrow, then I shall still plant a tree today." It is quite remarkable the way she juxtaposed these disjoined pieces and made it all come together to make sense. I especially like the bright red accents and I love the showy split leaf philodendron patch at the bottom. I wish I could plan works in a similar way.

Herta would love to have the term, "reverse appliqué," abolished completely. She uses the singular term, "appliqué," to cover the methods she uses. While doing research at the Victoria and Albert Museum in London, she found a publication entitled *Notes of Applied Work and Patchwork*. In describing "applied work," it makes a brief vague reference to "the reserved technique," stating that "the shape and color is created by the ground material." It makes one wonder if through the years an original term, "reserve appliqué" became "reverse appliqué." Could it be that the "s" and "v" were transposed?

Each of us has his or her own style. I am sure if you try the techniques in this book and develop your own ways of interpreting them, many innovative ideas will flow.

■ **PHOTO 7-10.**
LET'S PLANT A TREE, 29" x 75", Herta Puls, 1992.
PHOTO: MICHAEL WICKS

PHOTO 7-10

73

CHAPTER 8

DESIGNING & QUILTING MOLA APPLIQUÉ

PHOTO 8-1

DESIGNING

Perhaps you want to try designing your own mola figures, motifs, or geometric patterns, or you want to do abstract fabric art. I often find that students have ideas for designs, but have no idea how to draw them. You may want to adapt an idea from a book, photograph, greeting card, or other source. The important thing to remember is to keep the design simple. So often people want to do something too complicated and get discouraged because the detail is just not workable. Deciding what to omit is more difficult than deciding what to include. Tiny detail is not possible.

I recommend that you first try working a few of the patterns in this book before trying to design your own. Then you will have a better understanding of the technique and its limitations.

Most mola designs begin with a channel. Therefore I always think in terms of working a channel when I think of a design. I design in two ways: using ¼" graph paper and a wide nib felt pen, and using a computer.

I find that using a wide nib felt pen keeps me from drawing a design that has too much fine detail. Using a fine pointed pen or pencil often results in getting bogged down with tiny detail. If you can draw a line with a wide point pen, then you can probably appliqué it as a channel.

When I design a pattern for a triple-outline channel, I draw my lines about ½" in width. This line accommodates a ¼" channel with two ⅛" edges.

Graph paper is helpful in designing geometric patterns because it aids in getting the spacing even. When drawing figures or curved designs, I use graph paper and a wide nib pen, making sure the spaces between channels are at least ¼" wide to accommodate the folded under seam allowances (opposite). I refine my drawings by placing tracing paper over them, redrawing to improve them or to change the size.

If you have a computer with a drawing program, you can design much faster. You can select lines the width of your channels. It is easy to make squares, circles, ovals, and arcs. You can flip elements, rotate them and, best of all, repeat them. I do not find it very easy to do freehand drawing on the computer, but some computer drawing programs have tools that make this easier. I have always used a Macintosh® Plus (below), which at this point is outdated. I find it troublesome to approach an updated computer because I am so comfortable with the model I use. I use MacDraft® and Canvas® software to construct my designs.

As I described in Chapter 7, I usually experiment with a few mola blocks, trying designs and fabrics to make two or three blocks to see how they look. Then I decide how I will use them in a quilt. This can be a frustrating stage because I am anxious to proceed with more pieces, but I feel I must first decide on a direction to take. Sometimes it takes a long time to find a way to use my experimental pieces. I look through magazines; books on art, design, and quilts; and attend quilt shows for inspiration. Then suddenly an idea happens and I can proceed.

I often work out quilt designs on the computer. I draw the size of a block to scale, repeat it and then just play with it. I don't bother with detail of the block, just a basic idea for the layout of the quilt. I print the design, make a few changes, and print it again so I can compare several before I decide on the final approach. I don't worry about color at that point. Even with a color computer monitor, trying out the final fabric color is what matters.

QUILTING

This is the most challenging part for me. My mind goes blank when I am faced with the dilemma of how to quilt large spaces. When quilting the channels, it makes sense to make the quilt stitches down the middle of the channels. I like the look of it and this is the thinnest part of a design to push the needle through. I first tried quilting in the ditch along the two sides of the channel, but decided I preferred the look of quilting one line down the middle.

Quilting is not my strong point. I know there are many people who could take the designs I do and quilt them in a much more suitable way.

After I completed STUMBLING BLOCKS (page 66), I made up my mind to start machine quilting. I am still not capable of free motion machine quilting, but quilters who are very good at it would find quilting the channels of a mola design fairly easy. I have recently combined hand quilting with machine quilting to achieve the result I want. It may be a compromise, but it is up to each individual to work in the way best suited to his or her own temperament.

■ **PHOTO 8-1.**
Rough sketches for mola designs made with wide nib felt pen.

■ **PHOTO 8-2.**
Patterns for mola designs made on the computer.

PHOTO 8-2

PATTERNS

NOTE: Lines on the Primitive Critters and
Flowers Deco patterns indicate the cutting lines;
on the other patterns the lines represent the fold lines.

PATTERN A
Primitive Critters

cutting line

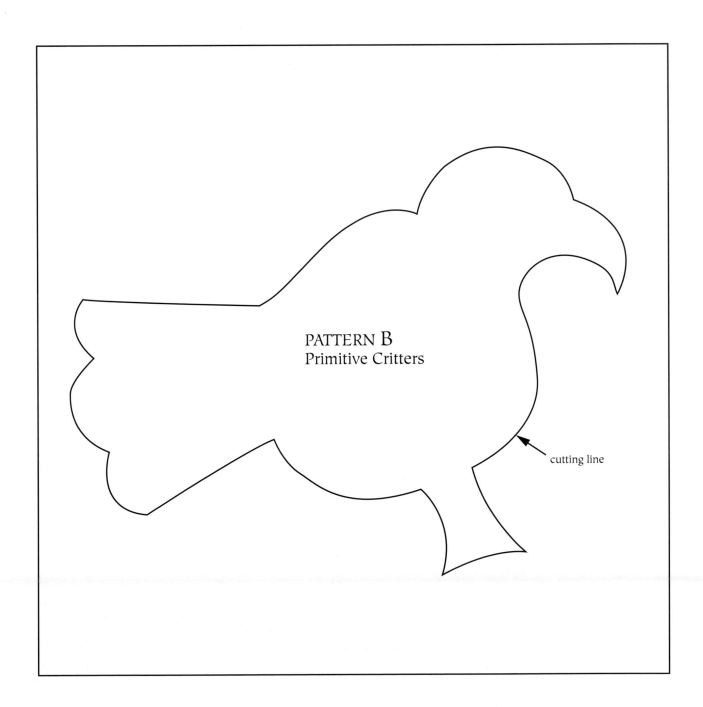

PATTERN B
Primitive Critters

cutting line

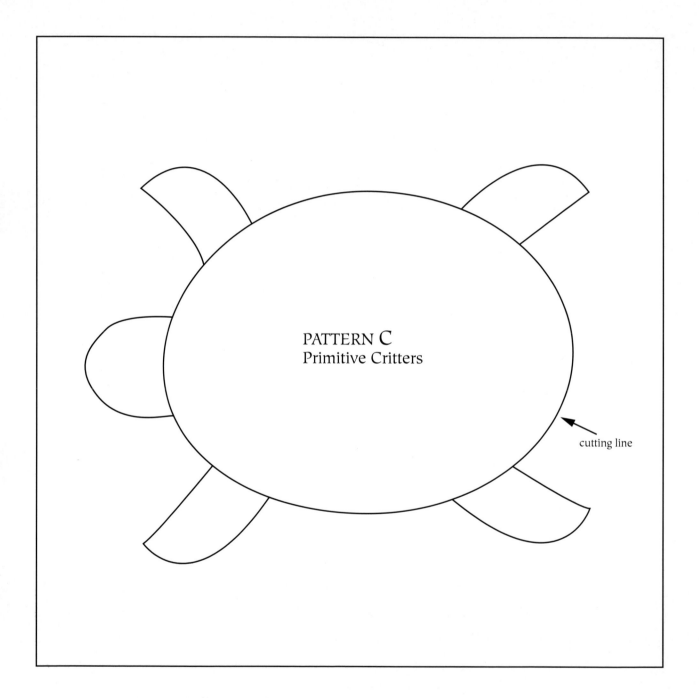

PATTERN C
Primitive Critters

cutting line

PATTERN D
Primitive Critters

cutting line

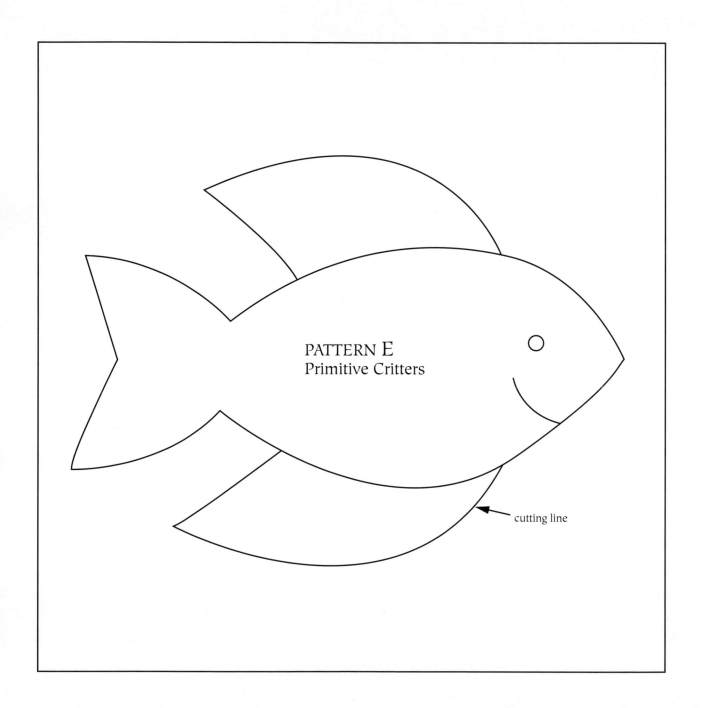

PATTERN E
Primitive Critters

cutting line

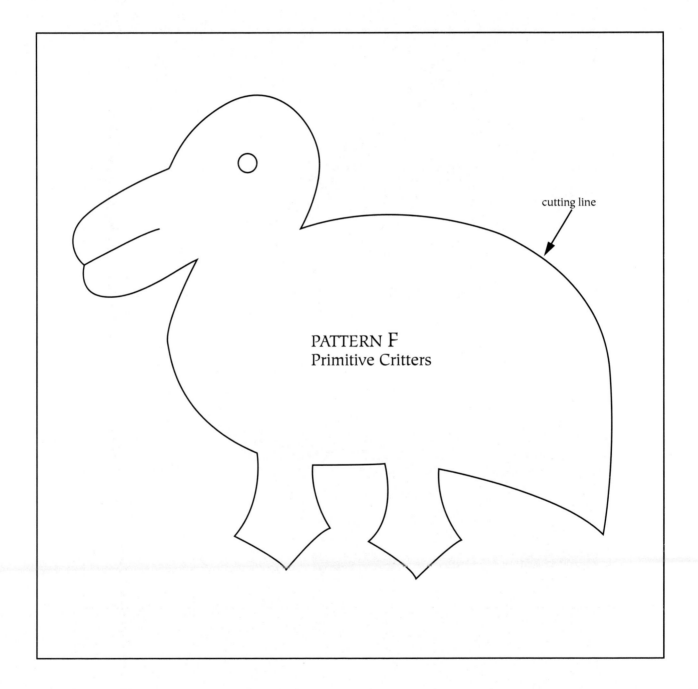

cutting line

PATTERN F
Primitive Critters

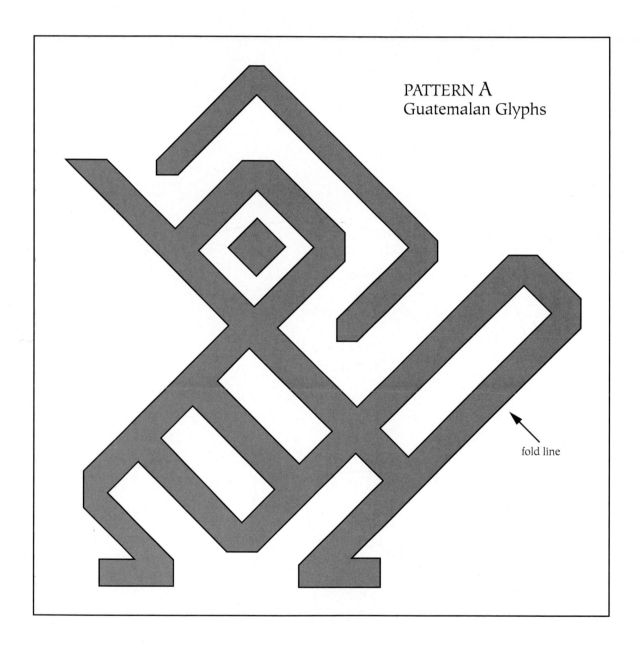

PATTERN A
Guatemalan Glyphs

fold line

PATTERN B
Guatemalan Glyphs

fold line

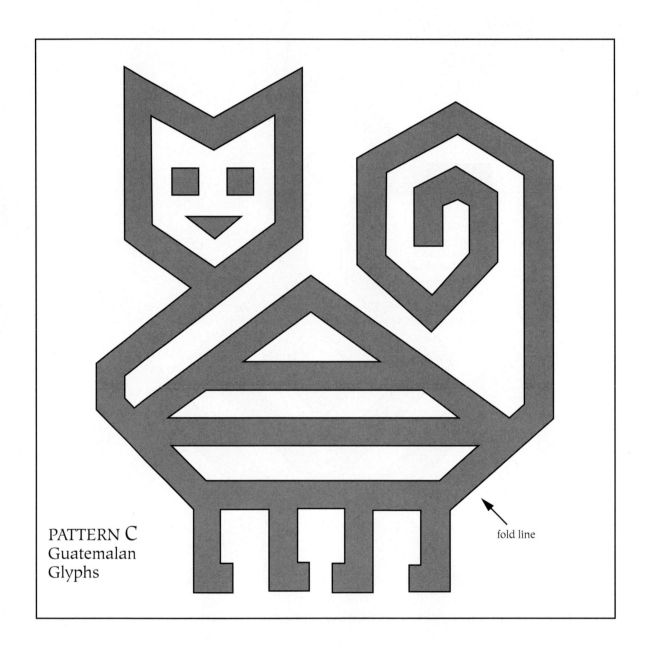

fold line

PATTERN C
Guatemalan
Glyphs

PATTERN D
Guatemalan Glyphs

fold line

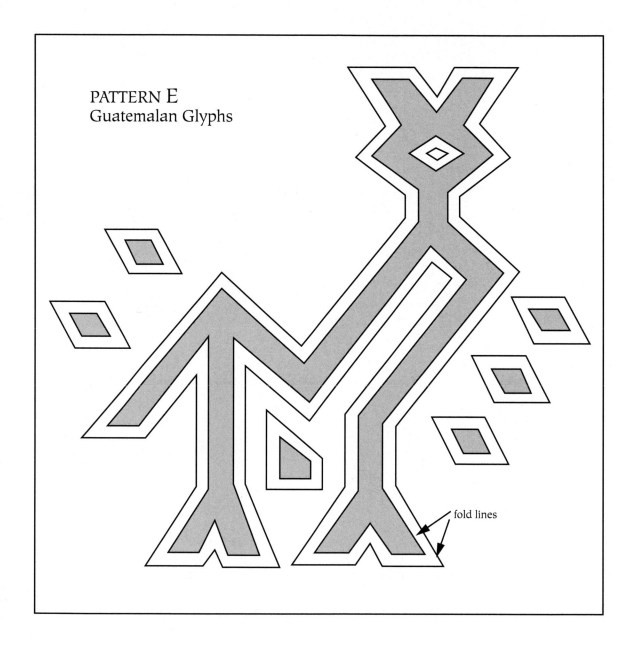

PATTERN E
Guatemalan Glyphs

fold lines

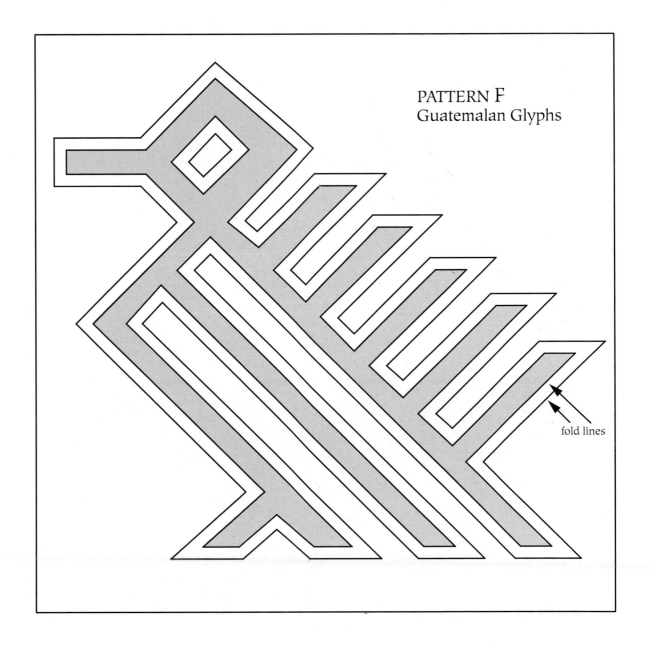

PATTERN F
Guatemalan Glyphs

fold lines

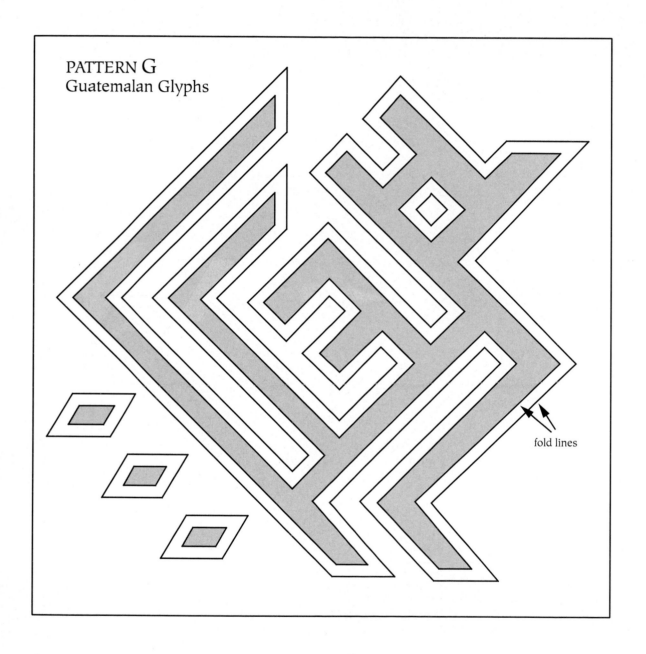

PATTERN G
Guatemalan Glyphs

fold lines

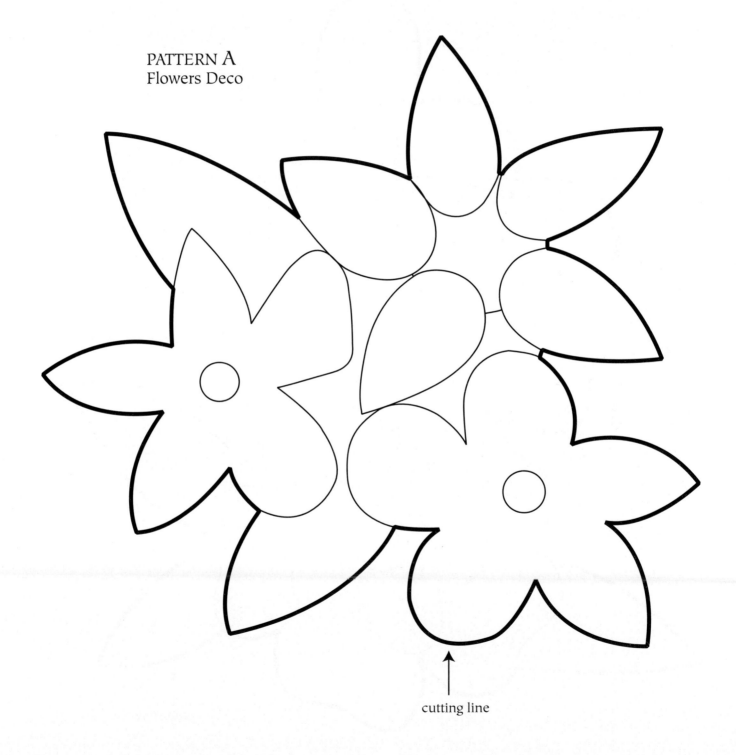

PATTERN A
Flowers Deco

cutting line

PATTERN B
Flowers Deco

cutting line

PATTERN C
Flowers Deco

cutting line

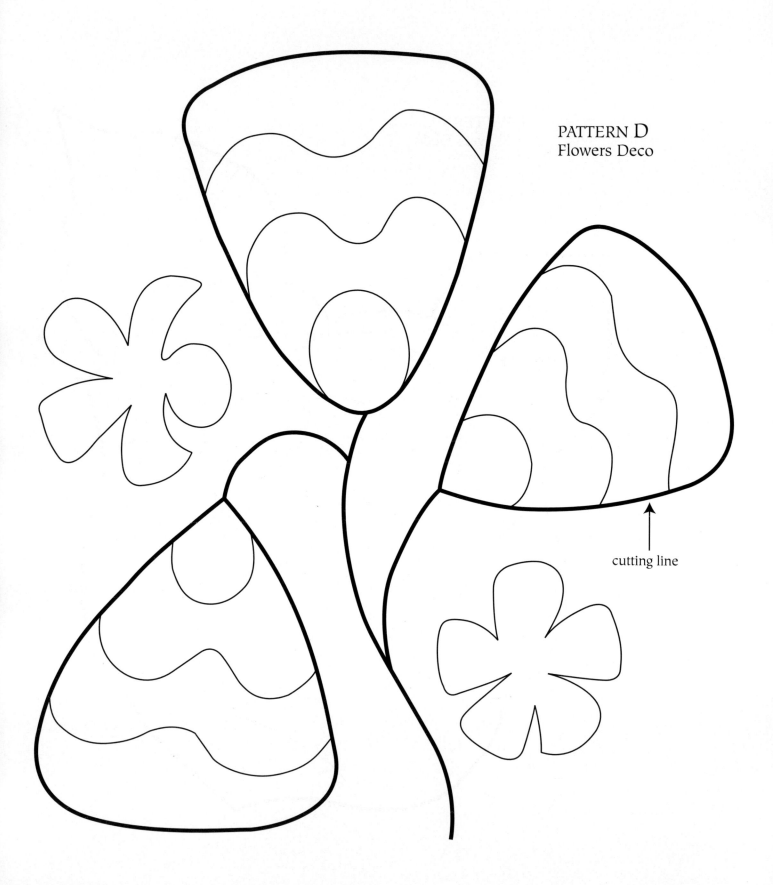

PATTERN D
Flowers Deco

cutting line

cutting line

PATTERN F
Flowers Deco

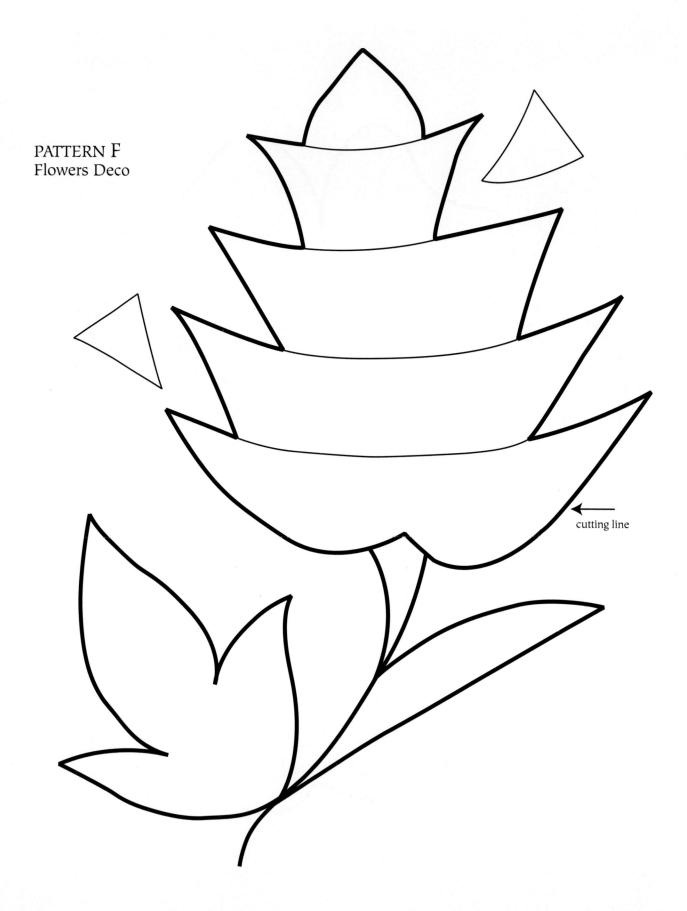

cutting line

PATTERN A
Repeat, Geometric
One outline

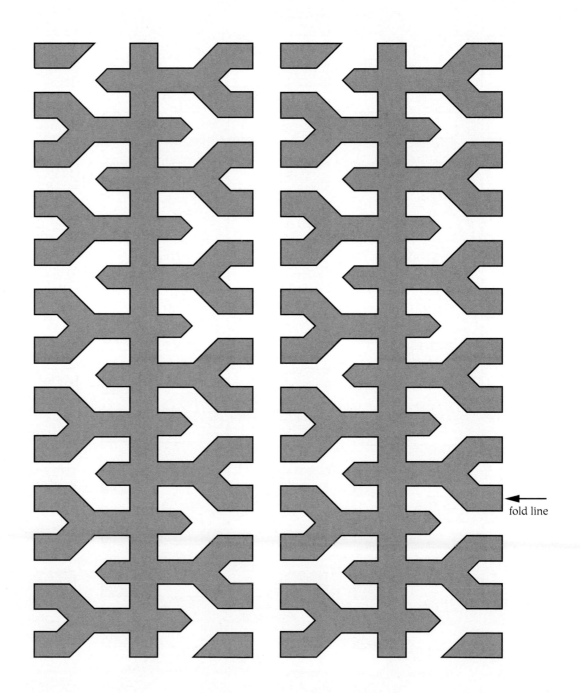

fold line

fold line

fold line

fold line

fold line

fold line

fold line

fold line

fold line

fold lines

fold lines

PATTERN J
Repeat, Geometric
Three outline

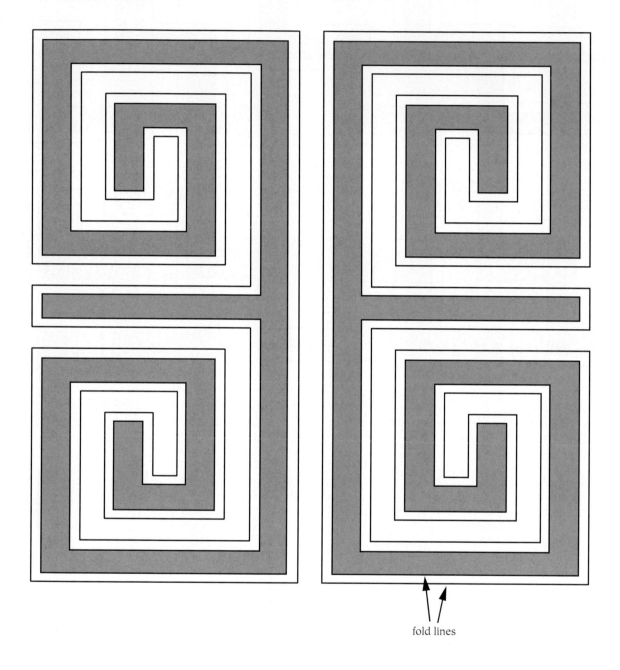

fold lines

PATTERN K
Repeat, Geometric
Three outline

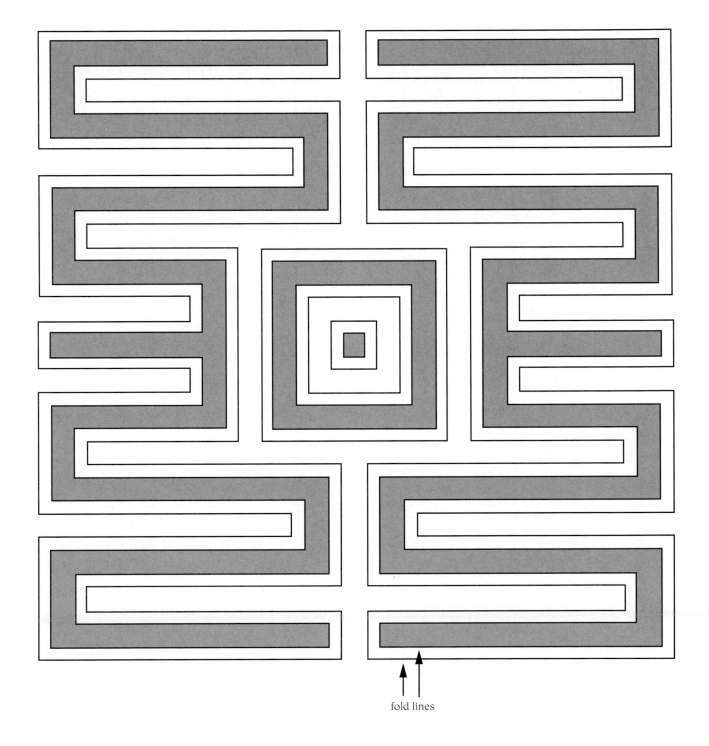

fold lines

PATTERN FOR
CHECKERBOARD
MOTIF

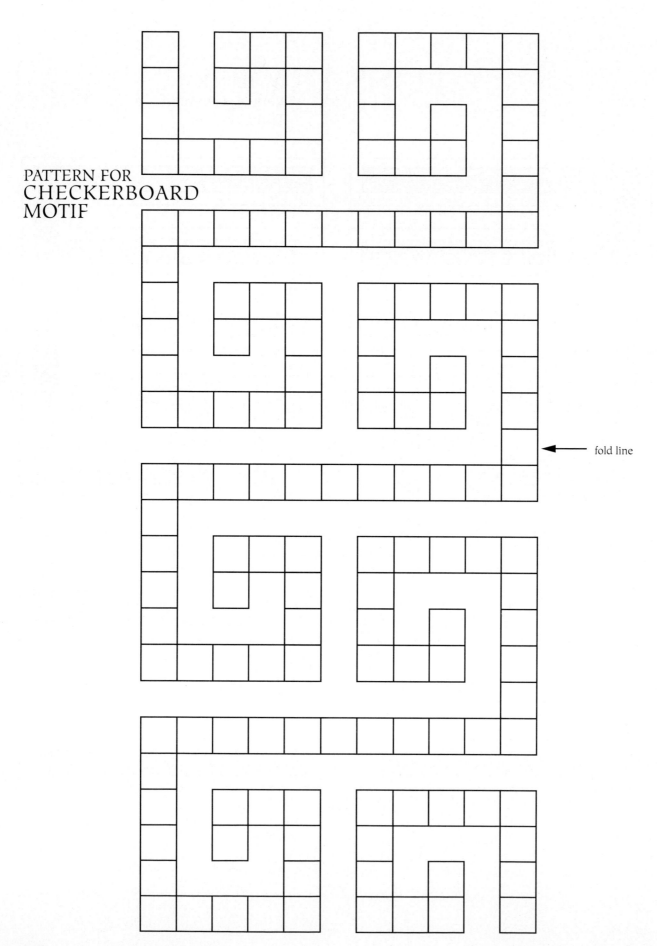

fold line

GLOSSARY

Baltimore Album: A special group of romantic appliquéd quilts, featuring flowers, trees, fruits, wreathes and baskets, with every block different, originally made in the Baltimore, Maryland area during the middle of the nineteenth century.

Base: The foundation layer of appliqué, also referred to as the underlayer or underneath fabric or layer.

Beam Compass: A compass with extra lengths that can be attached to create larger circles, used by draftsmen, artists and architects.

Celtic: Appliqué of ancient Celtic designs, featuring entwined bias strips, made popular by Philomena Durcan.

Channel Appliqué: Appliqué in which a slit is made in the top fabric, edges folded under and stitched to form a narrow groove or "channel", revealing the underneath fabric.

Cut-As-You-Go: A method of cutting appliqué a little at a time while stitching it, instead of precutting it.

Cutting Mat: A self-healing surface used for rotary cutting.

Cutting Ruler: Measuring tool of see-through plastic, available in many sizes as long rulers, squares and other conventient shapes, designed to work with rotary cutters.

Double Appliqué: Appliqué in which two shapes are cut, the top one cut slightly smaller than the lower one so that the lower one forms a narrow outline around the upper one.

Fingerpress: Folding a small part of an edge under and pressing it with fingers before stitching it.

Foundation: The lower fabric of the appliqué, also referred to as the underlayer, underneath layer or base fabric.

Gutcheon: A current brand name of fabric, innovated by Jeff Gutcheon, a known quilter.

Hmong: A hill tribe from Laos, Thailand and North Vietnam.

Hoffman: A current brand name manufacturer of innovative fabric.

Inlay Appliqué: In this book, appliqué in which the background is cut from the top layer to leave an opening or openings, revealing the underneath layer. Other shapes of the design are then inlaid within the openings, cut so that they interlock like jigsaw puzzle pieces. When stitched down, channels form an outline between the shapes.

Kuna Indians: Originators of the molas. (Kuna is also spelled Cuna.)

Lap Desk: Portable desk top, made as a box with compartments for supplies with a lid sloped for comfortable writing.

Light Box: A translucent drawing surface structured over a light source, used for tracing by draftsmen, artists, architects.

Molas: Blouses made and worn by the Kuna Indian women of the San Blas Islands of Panama. Also the panels of appliqué, seamed into the blouses.

Negative Appliqué: A type of appliqué, not as commonly used, in which the design is cut through the background so that it looks incised. Also called reverse appliqué.

Outline: Feature of most molas, made by creating narrow channels and by double appliqué.

Pa ndau: A form of appliqué needlework made by Hmong women of the highlands of Laos, Thailand and nearby countries. Very similar and often compared to some forms of molas. Also known as flower cloth.

Positive Appliqué: Appliqué, as it is best known, in which one or more patches are sewn to a foundation.

Positive and Negative Appliqué: The two main types of appliqué.

Quilting in the Ditch: Placing quilting stitches in the seam or adjacent to the edge of appliqué.

Reverse Appliqué: Appliqué in which an opening is cut in the upper layer and stitched to reveal the underneath layer so the design looks incised. Also called negative appliqué.

Rotary Cutter: A handy tool for cutting made with a very sharp round blade that cuts when rolled.

San Blas Islands: Home of the Kuna Indians off the Atlantic side of Panama.

Sawtooth Edge: A delicate feature of some molas, made to resemble rickrack.

Tandem Appliqué: Two or more appliqué designs, cut simultaneously, with the parts positioned over two or more foundations to make duplicate designs of varying color arrangements.

Un-Mola Appliqué: Narrow strips of appliqué in which each part is no wider than 1/8 or 1/4 inch in width, found frequently in Kuna Indian molas, unexpected by most who believe molas to be completely reverse appliqué.

Underlayer: The base, foundation or underneath layer of appliqué.

BIBLIOGRAPHY

Auld, Rhoda L. *Molas*. New York: Van Nostrand Reinhold, 1977.

Bath, Virginia Churchill. *Embroidery Masterworks*. Chicago, Illinois: Henry Regnery Co., 1972.

Billcliffe, Roger. *Charles Rennie Mackintosh Textile Designs*. Rohnert Park, California: Pomegranate Artbooks, 1993.

Browne, Lady Richmond. *Unknown Tribes Uncharted Seas*. London: Duckworth, 1924.

Carraway, Caren. *The Mola Design Coloring Book*. Owings Miles, Maryland: Stemmer House Publishers, Inc., 1981.

Iglesias, Marvel and Vandervelde, Marjorie. *Beauty is a Ring in my Nose?* Emmetsburg, Iowa: Velde Press, 1978.

____ *Born Primitive*. Emmetsburg, Iowa: Velde Press, 1982.

Kapp, Kit S. *Mola Art from the San Blas Islands*. Cincinnati, Ohio: K.S. Kapp Publications, 1972.

Keeler, Clyde E. *Cuna Indian Art*. New York, New York: Exposition Press, 1969.

Kelly, Joanne M. *Cuna*. South Brunswick, New Jersey, A.S. Barnes and Co., Inc., 1966.

Mann, John. *Siabibi's San Blas*. Colon, Republic of Panama: Siabibi S.A., Box 1997, 1975.

____ *Siabibi's Little Bird*. Colon, Republic of Panama, Siabibi S.A., Box 1997, 1978.

McAndrews, Anita. *Cuna Cosmology, Legends of Panama*. Collected and translated from Kuna into Spanish by Tomás Herrara Porras. Washington, District of Columbia and Shantih, Brooklyn, New York: Three Continents Press, 1978.

Parker, Ann and Neal, Avon. *Molas, Folk Art of the Cuna Indians*. Barre, Massachusetts: Barre Publishing, 1977.

Patera, Charlotte. *Cutwork Appliqué*. Piscataway, New Jersey: New Century Publishers, Inc., 1983.

____ *Mola Making*. Piscataway, New Jersey: New Century Publishers, Inc., 1984.

Puls, Herta. *Cutwork and Appliqué, Historic, Modern and Kuna Indians*. B. T. Batsford, 1978.

____ *Textiles of the Kuna Indians*. Aylsbury, Bucks, United Kingdom: Shire Publications Ltd., 1988.

Salvador, Mari Lyn. *Yar Dailege! Kuna Women's Art*. Albuquerque, New Mexico: The Maxwell Museum of Anthropology, The University of New Mexico, 1978.

Shaffaer, Frederick S. *Mola Design Coloring Book*. New York, Dover Publications, Inc., 1982.

Wade, David. *Geometric Patterns and Borders*. New York, New York: Van Nostrand Reinhold, 1982.

Williams, Geoffrey. *African Designs from Traditional Sources*. New York, New York: Dover Publishing, Inc., 1971.

Note: Kuna is also spelled Cuna

INDEX

~American Quilter's Society~

dedicated to publishing books for today's quilters

The following AQS publications are currently available:

- **Adapting Architectural Details for Quilts,** Carol Wagner, #2282: AQS, 1992, 88 pages, softbound, $12.95
- **American Beauties: Rose & Tulip Quilts,** Gwen Marston & Joe Cunningham, #1907: AQS, 1988, 96 pages, softbound, $14.95
- **Appliqué Designs: My Mother Taught Me to Sew,** Faye Anderson, #2121: AQS, 1990, 80 pages, softbound, $12.95
- **Appliqué Patterns from Native American Beadwork Designs,** Dr. Joyce Mori, #3790: AQS, 1994, 96 pages, softbound, $14.95
- **Arkansas Quilts: Arkansas Warmth,** Arkansas Quilter's Guild, Inc., #1908: AQS, 1987, 144 pages, hardbound, $24.95
- **The Art of Hand Appliqué,** Laura Lee Fritz, #2122: AQS, 1990, 80 pages, softbound, $14.95
- **...Ask Helen More About Quilting Designs,** Helen Squire, #2099: AQS, 1990, 54 pages, 17 x 11, spiral-bound, $14.95
- **Award-Winning Quilts & Their Makers, Vol. I: The Best of AQS Shows – 1985-1987,** #2207: AQS, 1991, 232 pages, softbound, $24.95
- **Award-Winning Quilts & Their Makers, Vol. II: The Best of AQS Shows – 1988-1989,** #2354: AQS, 1992, 176 pages, softbound, $24.95
- **Award-Winning Quilts & Their Makers, Vol. III: The Best of AQS Shows – 1990-1991,** #3425: AQS, 1993, 180 pages, softbound, $24.95
- **Award-Winning Quilts & Their Makers, Vol. IV: The Best of AQS Shows – 1992-1993,** #3791: AQS, 1994, 180 pages, softbound, $24.95
- **Celtic Style Floral Appliqué: Designs Using Interlaced Scrollwork,** Scarlett Rose, #3926: AQS, 1995, 128 pages, softbound, $14.95
- **Classic Basket Quilts,** Elizabeth Porter & Marianne Fons, #2208: AQS, 1991, 128 pages, softbound, $16.95
- **A Collection of Favorite Quilts,** Judy Florence, #2119: AQS, 1990, 136 pages, softbound, $18.95
- **Creative Machine Art,** Sharee Dawn Roberts, #2355: AQS, 1992, 142 pages, 9 x 9, softbound, $24.95
- **Dear Helen, Can You Tell Me?...All About Quilting Designs,** Helen Squire, #1820: AQS, 1987, 51 pages, 17 x 11, spiral-bound, $12.95
- **Double Wedding Ring Quilts: New Quilts from an Old Favorite,** #3870: AQS, 1994, 112 pages, softbound, $14.95
- **Dye Painting!,** Ann Johnston, #3399: AQS, 1992, 88 pages, softbound, $19.95
- **Dyeing & Overdyeing of Cotton Fabrics,** Judy Mercer Tescher, #2030: AQS, 1990, 54 pages, softbound, $9.95
- **Encyclopedia of Pieced Quilt Patterns,** compiled by Barbara Brackman, #3468: AQS, 1993, 552 pages, hardbound, $34.95
- **Fabric Postcards: Landmarks & Landscapes • Monuments & Meadows,** Judi Warren, #3846: AQS, 1994, 120 pages, softbound, $22.95
- **Flavor Quilts for Kids to Make: Complete Instructions for Teaching Children to Dye, Decorate & Sew Quilts,** Jennifer Amor, #2356: AQS, 1991, 120 pages, softbound, $12.95
- **From Basics to Binding: A Complete Guide to Making Quilts,** Karen Kay Buckley, #2381: AQS, 1992, 160 pages, softbound, $16.95
- **Fun & Fancy Machine Quiltmaking,** Lois Smith, #1982: AQS, 1989, 144 pages, softbound, $19.95
- **Heirloom Miniatures,** Tina M. Gravatt, #2097: AQS, 1990, 64 pages, softbound, $9.95
- **Infinite Stars,** Gayle Bong, #2283: AQS, 1992, 72 pages, softbound, $12.95
- **The Ins and Outs: Perfecting the Quilting Stitch,** Patricia J. Morris, #2120: AQS, 1990, 96 pages, softbound, $9.95
- **Irish Chain Quilts: A Workbook of Irish Chains & Related Patterns,** Joyce B. Peaden, #1906: AQS, 1988, 96 pages, softbound, $14.95
- **Jacobean Appliqué: Book I, "Exotica,"** Patricia B. Campbell & Mimi Ayars, Ph.D, #3784: AQS, 1993, 160 pages, softbound, $18.95
- **The Judge's Task: How Award-Winning Quilts Are Selected,** Patricia J. Morris, #3904: AQS, 1993, 128 pages, softbound, $19.95
- **Marbling Fabrics for Quilts: A Guide for Learning & Teaching,** Kathy Fawcett & Carol Shoaf, #2206: AQS, 1991, 72 pages, softbound, $12.95
- **More Projects and Patterns: A Second Collection of Favorite Quilts,** Judy Florence, #3330: AQS, 1992, 152 pages, softbound, $18.95
- **Nancy Crow: Quilts and Influences,** Nancy Crow, #1981: AQS, 1990, 256 pages, 9 x 12, hardcover, $29.95
- **Nancy Crow: Work in Transition,** Nancy Crow, #3331: AQS, 1992, 32 pages, 9 x 10, softbound, $12.95
- **New Jersey Quilts – 1777 to 1950: Contributions to an American Tradition,** The Heritage Quilt Project of New Jersey; text by Rachel Cochran, Rita Erickson, Natalie Hart & Barbara Schaffer, #3332: AQS, 1992, 256 pages, softbound, $29.95
- **No Dragons on My Quilt,** Jean Ray Laury with Ritva Laury & Lizabeth Laury, #2153: AQS, 1990, 52 pages, hardcover, $12.95
- **Old Favorites in Miniature,** Tina Gravatt, #3469: AQS, 1993, 104 pages, softbound, $15.95
- **A Patchwork of Pieces: An Anthology of Early Quilt Stories 1845-1940,** complied by Cuesta Ray Benberry and Carol Pinney Crabb, #3333: AQS, 1993, 360 pages, 5½ x 8½, softbound, $14.95
- **Precision Patchwork for Scrap Quilts, Anytime, Anywhere...,** Jeannette Muir, #3928: AQS, 1995, 72 pages, softbound, $12.95
- **Quilt Groups Today: Who They Are, Where They Meet, What They Do, and How to Contact Them – A Complete Guide for 1992-1993,** #3308: AQS, 1992, 336 pages, softbound, $14.95
- **Quilter's Registry,** Lynne Fritz, #2380: AQS, 1992, 80 pages, 5½ x 8½, hardbound, $9.95
- **Quilting Patterns from Native American Designs,** Dr. Joyce Mori, #3467: AQS, 1993, 80 pages, softbound, $12.95
- **Quilting With Style: Principles for Great Pattern Design,** Gwen Marston & Joe Cunningham, #3470: AQS, 1993, 192 pages, hardbound, $24.95
- **Quiltmaker's Guide: Basics & Beyond,** Carol Doak, #2284: AQS, 1992, 208 pages, softbound, $19.95
- **Quilts: The Permanent Collection – MAQS,** #2257: AQS, 1991, 100 pages, 10 x 6½, softbound, $9.95
- **Roots, Feathers & Blooms: 4-Block Quilts, Their History & Patterns, Book I,** Linda Giesler Carlson, #3789: AQS, 1994, 128 pages, softbound, $16.95
- **Seasons of the Heart & Home: Quilts for a Winter's Day,** Jan Patek, #3796: AQS, 1993, 160 pages, softbound, $18.95
- **Seasons of the Heart & Home: Quilts for Summer Days,** Jan Patek, #3761: AQS, 1993, 160 pages, softbound, $18.95
- **Sensational Scrap Quilts,** Darra Duffy Williamson, #2357: AQS, 1992, 152 pages, softbound, $24.95
- **Sets & Borders,** Gwen Marston & Joe Cunningham, #1821: AQS, 1987, 104 pages, softbound, $14.95
- **Show Me Helen...How to Use Quilting Designs,** Helen Squire, #3375: AQS, 1993, 155 pages, softbound, $15.95
- **Somewhere in Between: Quilts and Quilters of Illinois,** Rita Barrow Barber, #1790: AQS, 1986, 78 pages, softbound, $14.95
- **Spike & Zola: Patterns for Laughter...and Appliqué, Painting, or Stenciling,** Donna French Collins, #3794: AQS, 1993, 72 pages, softbound, $9.95
- **Stenciled Quilts for Christmas,** Marie Monteith Sturmer, #2098: AQS, 1990, 104 pages, softbound, $14.95
- **The Stori Book of Embellishing: Great Ideas for Quilts and Garments,** Mary Stori, #3929: AQS, 1994, 96 pages, softbound, $16.95
- **Straight Stitch Machine Appliqué: History, Patterns & Instructions for This Easy Technique,** Letty Martin, #3903: AQS, 1994, 160 pages, softbound, $16.95
- **Striplate Piecing: Piecing Circle Designs with Speed and Accuracy,** Debra Wagner, #3792: AQS, 1994, 168 pages 9 x 12, hardbound, $24.95
- **Tessellations and Variations: Creating One-Patch & Two-Patch Quilts,** Barbara Ann Caron, #3930: AQS, 1994, 120 pages, softbound, $14.95
- **Three-Dimensional Appliqué and Embroidery Embellishment: Techniques for Today's Album Quilt,** Anita Shackelford, #3788: AQS, 1993, 152 pages, 9 x 12, hardbound, $24.95
- **Time-Span Quilts: New Quilts from Old Tops,** Becky Herdle, #3931: AQS, 1994, 136 pages, softbound, $16.95
- **A Treasury of Quilting Designs,** Linda Goodmon Emery, #2029: AQS, 1990, 80 pages, 14 x 11, spiral-bound, $14.95
- **Tricks with Chintz: Using Large Prints to Add New Magic to Traditional Quilt Blocks,** Nancy S. Breland, #3847: AQS, 1994, 96 pages, softbound, $14.95
- **Wonderful Wearables: A Celebration of Creative Clothing,** Virginia Avery, #2286: AQS, 1991, 184 pages, softbound, $24.95

These books can be found in local bookstores and quilt shops. If you are unable to locate a title in your area, you can order by mail from AQS, P.O. Box 3290, Paducah, KY 42002-3290. Please add $1 for the first book and 40¢ for each additional one to cover postage and handling. (International orders please add $1.50 for the first book and $1 for each additional one.)